FAITH: FULL CIRCLE

The Religious Journey of a Baby-boomer Afrikaner

Bruwer Swanepoel

Copyright © 2021 Bruwer Swanepoel

ISBN 978-0-6397-8103-7

Proofreading & editing: Yvonne Shapiro
Typesetting & editing: Leah Marais
Image researcher: Sarie Potter
Cover concept: Nelmarie Swanepoel
Cover artwork: Sally Rumball
Cover design: Adam Rumball, Sharkbuoys Designs

Publisher: Self-published by Bruwer Swanepoel

All rights reserved. No part of this publication may be reproduced in any form or by any means, including photocopying or any information storage or retrieval system, without written permission from the publisher.

Disclaimer: Every reasonable effort has been made to trace the copyright holders of images reproduced in this publication. The publisher/author would be grateful for any information on copyright holders not credited or credited incorrectly. These errors will be rectified in any future editions.

Endorsements

FAITH: FULL CIRCLE is the fascinating life story of how and why the author had cultivated an intense religious conviction and then, slowly and hesitantly, had grown out of that conviction again. Characteristics of a creative mind are at play here: an inquisitive nature and a persistent desire to explore limits and test boundaries. It could be seen as two stories, brilliantly interwoven as a métissage. The religious journey's full circle is completed and confirmed by thrilling evolutionary and scientific observations.
– Antoinette le Roux, PhD and wife of a former minister of the Dutch Reformed Church

A personal goal of enlightenment, a pursuit of knowledge to understand the human condition and reason for existence, is often left unexplored by the unquestioning nature of the Afrikaner. As the author traces his history and outlines his exploration of different ideas, he breaks with this Afrikaner tradition. In his search for the truth about his God and religion, he embraces personal growth, enthusiasm, and acceptance of his journey of self-exploration. He may be criticised for casting himself into another role as an atheist at the conclusion of the book. However, such criticism would be unfounded since he has left his unquestioning roots behind and has explored and acquired a role of his own choice.
– Maylene Swiegers, PhD

There are bags full of wisdom and humour in this narration.
– Professor Izak Spangenberg, PhD, Emeritus Professor (Old Testament) University of South Africa

An Afrikaner recalls episodes in his life, questions and analyses doctrine and invokes thought. A thoroughly researched, lucid and fascinating read.
– Mark Manthe, PhD

*Dedicated to the friends I alienated and lost,
as well as to the friends I gained,
as a result of my journey.*

*Written when the lockdown forced us to slow down during the
Covid-19 pandemic in the year of the Lord, 2020/21*

Contents

Preface	**vii**
Chapter 1: When I was very young	1
My pre-school and primary school days	
My grandmother	
My first church experiences	
Chapter 2: When I was a little older	6
My secondary school and hostel days	
My mother	
My first conversion	
The first highlight of my faith career	
My church experiences in Europe	
Chapter 3: In my early adult years	14
My year in the army	
My years at university	
The alliance between state and religion	
Films, books and plays	
My first faith-healing experience	
Chapter 4: In my middle years	28
The start of my working career	
My father	
My church life in two congregations	
The second highlight of my faith career	
The Gideons International	
The third highlight of my faith career	
God revealed to me proof of the afterlife	
Chapter 5: In my later years (when my faith started to falter)	38
I walked the Via Dolorosa in Jerusalem	
The promises of God in the Bible	
The first turning point in my faith career	
Content in the Bible	
The second turning point in my faith career	
My second faith-healing experience	
LitNet and the Nuwe Hervorming Netwerk	
My second conversion	

Chapter 6: In my final years (when my faith finally died)   56

Discovering history and evolution
A brief history of humankind
The history of everything
Language took Homo sapiens to the top of the food chain
Homo sapiens created fictional storytelling
Languages in nature
The agricultural revolution and some consequences

Beginnings and evolving life on Earth
A definition of life
The first replicator
God creating Samurai crabs
Something about brain evolution

Chapter 7: Where I am today (what is left of my final years)   95

My journey continues

The scientific backdrop
Forever-ness in an evolving universe
The Second Law of Thermodynamics
The God-of-the-Gaps
The interconnectedness of everything
The Big Bang and the forming of stars
God creating the atomic elements
Supernovas and black holes

The religious backdrop
Religion outside of the Bible
The Gospel of Judas
The first image of God
Origins of the religious impulse

Conclusion
Meaning and purpose of life
Religion and morality

References and notes	136
Image credits	138
Acknowledgements	139
Index	141

Preface

If you live intensely and pursue your goals with passion, you risk falling into traps of obsession because you have the propensity to overcook things. I have been there and done that more than once in my life. In this instance, my infatuation was with religion. I engaged with religion when I was in my teens, and over many years it became an absorbing journey of search and discovery. I would submit that the searching and discovering were related to my love of reading. I am and always was, an avid reader. A good case can be made to conclude that it was reading that guided me into faith, as well as out of faith.

I learned early in my life to find my way and make things work for myself. My grandmother was the guiding light in my life for a significant part of my formative years. I am neither an extrovert nor an introvert, but I can be very social and competitive; I suspect that, as a teenager, it was peer pressure that initially guided me to the church. Parental instruction was not the motivation.

After that, my circumstances and environment played the leading roles in keeping me devoted to the church and growing my faith. During my secondary school years, the discipline of hostel life took care of church attendance, twice on any given Sunday. My conversion moment in the hospital at the age of sixteen left a meaningful impression and lasted a very long time. My mother became the motivating force in my life. My first exposure to a world outside of South Africa opened my eyes to religious diversity, and these impressions have lasted a lifetime.

The pact I made with God during my conscript year in the army kept my faith alive. Pretoria is a conservative Afrikaner environment where religion is a substantial part of the social order. My years at Tukkies (the University of Pretoria) reflected this, and my faith survived varsity life unscathed. Because of my inquisitive nature, I grasped, already in my early years in South Africa, a sense of the unholy alliance between state and religion. In my later years, my corporate career enabled me to work in different countries, and I experienced this partnership everywhere in the world and also in Russia and the United States. My constant desire to explore limits and test boundaries led me to watch movies, attend performances and read books frowned upon in my homeland at the time when I backpacked through Europe in the 1974/75 winter season. Even though my faith was growing, my sceptic brain was always present – and never more emphatically than during my first exposure to faith healing. Even so, in my later years, I succumbed again, and this time, I even agreed to be the patient.

As a bursary holder, I started my working career with the South African Railways in January 1976. We lived in Hillbrow, Johannesburg, and joined the Irene congregation of the Dutch Reformed Church in Doornfontein. In 1978 we relocated to Kempton Park and became members of the Edleen congregation. My religious journey grew in leaps and bounds during this time. I studied the Bible with total surrender and worked through dozens of Biblecor courses and other Biblical literature in pursuing my zeal to grow in my faith. I was comprehensively involved in the structures of the church for twenty-five years. I completed a two-year course on the "Unique Message of the Bible" under the auspices of the

University of Pretoria. I joined The Gideons International in 1990, served as President of the Kempton Park camp for three consecutive years, and was intensely committed to their cause for fifteen years. I delved deep into the Word of God, and God revealed to me mathematical proof of the afterlife. I shared "my revelation" in Bible study groups and at Gideon dinner meetings, and it was always well received.

My expectations were high, and I desperately wanted my faith to work, to be alive and to make a difference. I walked the Via Dolorosa in Jerusalem (1999) in search of what it meant to follow in the footsteps of Jesus. I came back from Israel with more questions than answers. My fascination with the rational and personal God of the Bible led me to evaluate the content of the Bible critically, and some of it became a distraction for me. I took the Trinity God at his Word and tested him on his promises, and I was disappointed. I then learned that I was not alone and by far not the only Afrikaner baby boomer questioning the status quo and the prevailing religious wisdom in South Africa at the time (2003/04). There was an unexpected explosion of opinions in Afrikaans newspapers and on LitNet, the Afrikaner portal of the emerging internet, on the topic of the existence of God. In the end, my second conversion was a non-event because it was long in the making, and it came cautiously and hesitantly.

I retired from the corporate world in September 2016 and had a great deal more time for reading and discovering. This part of my journey started with finding what I call "the history of everything", as summarised by Yuval Noah Harari in his book *Sapiens: A Brief History of Humankind.*[1] I learned how modern humans (*Homo sapiens*), since our inception into the world of species, moved up the ladder to occupy the top spot in the food chain in a breathtakingly short time. How *Homo sapiens* created fiction and how their fictional stories, over millennia, continuously change to adapt to the realities of the time, including their image of God.

I then discovered evolution, which opened up a most fantastic and thrilling world of wonder. I read widely about it from more than one scientific perspective. I learned about the incredible beauty of natural selection over unfathomable time scales, about the beginnings of life and the fascinating replicating molecule. My conviction that the rational and personal God of the Bible does not exist was confirmed. I not only felt relieved and vindicated but also empowered, and started feeling comfortable with my developing agnostic views. I learned how life on Earth simply oozed for around 3 billion years, but then about 500 million years ago; it started to grow leaves, trunks, gills, wings, arms, legs and eyes.

My journey continues and is becoming increasingly captivating. I am starting to learn something about the spectacular wonder of our universe – an evolving universe that makes stars, and stars that make star systems (planets and moons), and star systems that make galaxies. I am learning about Supernovas and black holes and how so much of this is explained by science today. The God-of-the-Gaps is losing legitimacy, as science is progressively closing the knowledge gaps. I am learning how everything in the universe is interconnected and how everything on Earth consists of stardust, including us.

I have started reading scholarly books on religious history and realised why and how inevitable it was that man had created God in his image and not the other way around. I am learning something about the possible origins of the religious impulse and why the God-image incessantly changes. It all confirms my conviction of the status of the Trinity God of the Bible. I have come to think of myself as a free-thinking individual, not bound by superstition or indoctrination.

1

When I was very young

I was born in Pretoria in September 1951 and, for the first four or five years of my life, lived with my parents, younger brother and sister in a face-brick house with a corrugated iron roof in Willies Hill Street, Pretoria Gardens. All the houses were face-brick and had corrugated iron roofs, so all looked the same, and none stood out. The road in front of our house was a dirt road, and it was the last road in the suburb, with a wide-open veld at the back, which allowed us a universe of space to roam and explore. Like most other parents in our suburb, my parents were both full-time working people, and we only saw them in the early mornings and late afternoons. Life was a paradise with so much open space and freedom. We were typical young baby boomers enjoying life under the African sun with little supervision and lots of friends, discovering, exploring, experimenting and making things work for ourselves.

Most of the households in our little environment were Afrikaner households, and many of the people worked for either the government or semi-government institutions and municipalities. Thinking back, it is fair to say that, on average, English-speaking, private-sector and entrepreneurial Afrikaners did not live in Pretoria Gardens.

My father joined the police force when he was sixteen years

old and retired from it in 1983 when he was fifty-eight. When he retired, he sold the house and bought a small farm, with a dilapidated stone house on it near Skeerpoort, against the foothills of the Magaliesberg. My father grew up on a farm and had always wanted to return to tilling the soil and raising animals. My mother was a bank clerk all her life until circumstances forced her to retire at around sixty. She, however, true to her innovative and entrepreneurial self, continued doing this and that, to put much-needed money on a bare table. My father died in 2003, and my mother got a new lease on life until she passed away in October 2018 at eighty-seven years of age. She was a special woman and a fun person, always brimming with positiveness and enthusiasm and sucking the marrow out of the little life she had. She taught us to dance when we could hardly walk, smoked till the day she died and never refused a glass of red wine. She made it work for the family and created the opportunities we had.

For reasons I only learned and understood later in my life, I lived with my grandmother in Ficksburg in the then Orange Free State province between the ages of five and nine. When I started my school career in 1958, Ficksburg was a tiny farming town, but already famous for its cherry farming. Ficksburg is situated on the banks of the Caledon River, today known as the Mohokare River, and the boundary with neighbouring Lesotho. My younger brother initially came with me, but at some stage returned to Pretoria to live with my mother and sister. So I started my school career at Ficksburg Volkskool, completing Sub A, Sub B, Standard One and Standard Two (these days Grades One, Two, Three, and Four) there. These were formative years in my life. I never knew my grandfather, as he died of a heart condition early in his life. My grandmother raised and took care of four children: my mother, two younger daughters and a late-arrival son, and then also a grandson.

She managed the only two cafés in Ficksburg in those days. The one café was in town and the other at the railway station. Sadly, for many years now – like in so many other country farming towns in South Africa today – no trains are running through Ficksburg anymore, and the railway station is derelict. My grandmother was hands-on involved at both cafés during any given day of a seven-day week, walking back and forth between them to do whatever was required. She was a hard worker. She always worked. I cannot remember my grandmother ever taking a holiday or a day off, taking a break, relaxing or having any kind of fun. She was always busy doing something useful.

The cafés belonged to, and my grandmother worked for, Mr Sorour, the "Jew of the town", as he was referred to in those days. We lived in the same building as the café in town. The building belonged to Mr Sorour, as did many other buildings in town. Reflecting back, I can say without any doubt that I never heard a single negative word or comment about Mr Sorour ever uttered by my grandmother. I would say that the respect that this old lady had and showed towards her prominent employer, landlord and benefactor, had a significant impact on my view of Jewish people in the later years of my life. I should add that as far as I can remember, the respect was mutual. She lived to ninety-four years of age and died quietly one day without, as far as I know, ever being sick.

I contracted meningitis when I was six years old. Although my recollection is vague, I remember that I was in bed, either in the hospital or at home, for many months. I was extremely weak even after having recuperated; it took some weeks for me to learn to walk and run again. However, what stayed with me was the times I woke up and saw my grandmother on her knees next to my bed, praying for my recovery. I went to Sunday school with my friends but cannot remember attending church services with my grandmother. I think she was just too busy working. I remember the years in Ficksburg as a good phase of my life. I did not miss my parental home. My grandmother was a disciplined woman and strict, but there was peace in the house. My grandmother's late-arrival son, my uncle, was ten years older than me, and he and his friends had a significant influence on the development of a five-to-nine-year-old boy. Not necessarily always wholesome and good, but life was exciting with much freedom and a lot to learn. Running with much bigger boys was a hard act, but it taught me to think for myself, fend for myself and take care of myself. In a sense, my uncle filled the roles of both a bigger brother and a father. More than once, he gave me a hiding with his cadet belt when I misbehaved, in his opinion. I could swim like a fish when I was six years old. We swam in the Caledon River and once witnessed the corpse of a drowned person being taken out of the river, but not before the crabs and other river occupants had started to eat on his lips and ears. I learned to shoot "bosduiwe" with an air gun. Afterwards, we would clean them and grill them on an open fire.

Against my wishes at the time, I then had to return to Pretoria. I moved back to my parents (who were together again after being separated for four years) and my brother and sister. We lived in a flat near the Pretoria West Power Station but moved to a two-bedroomed house just down the street when I was eleven. So, after finishing my first four primary school years at Ficksburg Volkskool in the Orange Free State, I attended Andries Pretorius Laerskool in central Pretoria for the last three years. My brother and I initially travelled to school by bus. However, we were given bicycles for Christmas 1963, and during my last year in primary school, we cycled the five kilometres to school, with my six-year-old sister – starting her school career – sitting askew on the bicycle frame in front of me.

I somehow developed an affinity for religion when I was eleven or twelve years old. It was during the last two years of my primary school days that I developed a desire to attend church services. I cannot say where this desire came from, but with hindsight am pretty sure it had to do with peer pressure.

Although my parents were believers and members of the local Dutch Reformed congregation wherever we happened to live, they were not regular church-going people, and religion was not dominant in our family life. I started to attend the Sunday morning church service and the Sunday school hour afterwards, together with my two best friends. They lived within walking distance of the church, but it was a bus ride away for me. I sometimes also attended the church services on Sunday evenings. I was twelve years old but distinctly remember a couple of times when my parents walked me to the Pretoria West bus station on a Sunday evening on my way to church and me walking back home alone from the station afterwards. I felt good about going to church twice on a Sunday.

2

When I was a little older

When the time came to move on to secondary school, my mother made another momentous decision as she decided it would be better for her children to attend school away from home, as residents in a school hostel. She decided on Hoërskool Brits, which had a reputable and above-average size secondary school hostel. Brits was a small but thriving farming town in the 1960s, northwest of the Hartbeespoort Dam and fifty-five kilometres from Pretoria. So in January of 1965, I checked in as a resident of the school hostel, courtesy of my mother. My five years of secondary school was another good phase in my life, and it was rounded off when I was elected head boy of the school and hostel in my matric (Grade Twelve) year, 1969.

Hostel life worked for me. Although I tend to push back on authority, I liked the routine and discipline of hostel life. Perhaps the "apprenticeship" under my uncle and his friends had also helped me cope and deal with life's challenges in a school hostel. I also valued the sense of independence it gave me. Besides, it suited my burgeoning affinity for religion. All hostel residents had to go to church, marching in a row from the hostel grounds to church and back, twice on any given Sunday. Every meal in the hostel dining room started with a prayer, and supper started with a passage from the Bible in addition to the prayer. All public schools (private schools were rare exceptions in South Africa in those days) had to adhere to the government policy of "Christian National Education". It entailed that all school children should be introduced to the Christian religion – especially the Protestant tradition. On Mondays, a minister from one of the Protestant churches would deliver a short sermon, which all school pupils were obliged to attend. The other days commenced with Bible reading and prayer done by the teachers in their respective classes. Pupils were expected to honour the headmaster and teachers as if they were their parents. Moreover, pupils were also expected to honour the rulers of the country and, in this way, become good citizens.

However, before pursuing further details of my religious journey during this phase in my life, I want to share an incident that may explain something about my propensity to test boundaries. Years later, my wife verbalised it differently by saying that I like to walk on the edge. Either way, in seeking excitement and fulfilment, I always seem to want to understand where the boundary limits are, in striving to make the most of every moment, situation or opportunity. And – if it is a cause and I believe in it – to pursue it with passion and total commitment. I can give many examples and better ones to prove the point, but I would instead share this one because it occurred early in my life, and it involved my mother:

It was Friday evening, 19 September 1969, and a couple of months before the class of '69 would start writing matric school exams. It was also the day of my eighteenth birthday. My matric hostel friends and I were sitting in the hostel garden after dinner, chatting and sharing ambitious plans for a new life awaiting us after the exams at the end of a school era that seemed to have lasted more than a lifetime. So, at some point, I suggested that we "slip out" later that evening, go into town and celebrate my last school birthday in style. The proposal was unanimously accepted, and later that evening, as soon as darkness fell, I recall that about twelve of us, the entire contingent of matrics in the residence that specific weekend, slipped out through the broken window, specifically "designed" for this purpose, and headed into town. Slipping out of the hostel was already breaking the rules, but venturing into town at night was a major transgression for hostel dwellers. Slipping out on mid-winter nights to visit surrounding orchards of oranges and naartjies could get you a good hiding and a note in your file. But slipping out and venturing into town, especially at night, was not only out of bounds, but a serious overreach for hostel students. So, here we were, twelve matric guys, running, singing and dancing down the main street of Brits, feeling and behaving as if we were on top of the world. We made enough noise to attract the attention of residents, who must have realised that we were hostel students out for a night of mischief. They called the hostel. If it had remained at that, no serious harm would have befallen us, but as we passed by the Brits Hotel, someone suggested a rest break, and so we entered the hotel, walked around to the garden at the back and ordered beers. If it had remained at that, again, no grave harm would have befallen us, but alas, after the round of beers, I could not resist the temptation to suggest a final round of drinks to crown an adventurous evening.

In the meantime, the teacher on hostel duty that evening was already driving through town looking for a bunch of noisy students. He did not find us because, at that stage, we were already at the back of the hotel in the garden. As fate would have it, this teacher liked his drink, and instead of driving through town searching for noisy students, he turned in at the hotel and sat down at the bar enjoying a nightcap. His unplanned visit to the hotel bar paid off handsomely for him. His interest was aroused when the outside waiter came in (for our second round of drinks), and placed an order at the bar, for what seemed to our teacher to be for at least a dozen serious drinkers. The order consisted of a variety of drinks, including vodka, lime & lemonade, brandy & coke, rum & coke and any other conceivable drink anyone has ever seen an adult enjoy. Our teacher, Mr Van Wyk, walked out with the waiter and confronted a bunch of chirpy and boisterous matric students, who were soon to turn very pale and worried. We never had our final round of drinks, and the piece of paper containing the drinks order was handed over to the Brits High School headmaster the very next day. To this day, I wonder who paid for the drinks that were never consumed – not by us at least. I was eighteen on that day and legally qualified to be served alcohol in public, but many of my mates were not. Our teacher may have pointed this fact out to a complaining bartender, i.e. serving alcohol to under-aged teenagers.

At six o'clock the next morning (Saturday morning!) I was pulled out of bed by the hostel headmaster, who was also the senior deputy headmaster of the secondary school, and was ordered to get my friends out of bed and meet him in his office. After explaining our side of the story as best as we could, we were marched to the headmaster in the "oval office". Here we had to explain every detail again, with not one of the teachers showing the slightest sign of empathy with our coming-of-age and innocent story. We were told to call home and ask our fathers to call the headmaster for an urgent appointment to come to Brits to meet with him. I called my mother that evening from the hostel's tickey box, and my first words were:

"Mom, I am in the shit!"

Her first words were:

"How deep, and what did you do?"

I related my side of the story and explained that the worst-case scenario was that I could be expelled from the hostel and maybe even from secondary school. What seemed inevitable was that I would be stripped of my honour colours received for academic, sport and cultural achievements over the past years, but more significantly would be stripped from my position as prefect and head boy. I was still busy explaining when my dear mother started to laugh and said:

"I'll see you Monday morning."

It took just over a week for all the parents to meet with the headmaster. My mother met with him twice. The details of what exactly was said, negotiated, promised and agreed were blurry, but the end result was six-of-the-best for each of us, and the rest was forgiven and forgotten. My mother established a reputation among the class of '69 hostel matrics that lasted a lifetime. Needless to say, I was quite proud of my mother.

I consider myself to be an all-round responsible person with a healthy respect for authority. However, I am curious, I probe, I query, and I challenge. I do not accept things at face value and tend to question conventional wisdom. For me, the authority must be deserved, must be legitimate, fair, result in compassionate outcomes, and improve not only my life but also that of the wider environment I live in; otherwise, the extent of that authority must be questioned. I believed in and was convinced of the authority claimed by the "Body of Christ" (the church), the Word of God (the Bible) and the triune God. Hence my intense religious journey. Maybe my expectations were too high, but we will come back to this.

I was sixteen years old when I contracted meningitis (the second time in my life) and spent some weeks in Pretoria General Hospital recovering from the illness. During the final phase (a week or two), while lying in a general ward after spending most of the time in isolation, a man appeared in the doorway, looked around the ward, and then approached an older man across the ward from me. A very short conversation followed, after which the man looked up, saw me looking at them, got up, came over to me, sat down next to my bed and asked me if I knew Jesus. I remembered saying yes, but when he prodded, and I did not give 'good' answers, he politely asked if he could explain the way to salvation. I was initially a bit shy, but then became curious and eventually thrilled to listen to him reading a few verses (from the Gospel of John) and explaining how easy the way to eternal salvation was. He then did for me what I did for many others, later on in my life: he held my hands and prayed with me and helped me to accept, in prayer, Jesus Christ as my personal Lord and Saviour. It was an overwhelming experience. Until a few years ago, I could even remember the exact date and the specific passage in the Bible that he shared with me. Many years later, after joining The Gideons International, I realised that the man who led me to become a "born-again Christian" was a Gideon.

I would say that this incident was the first highlight of my "faith career". About nine years later, when I started working and becoming more involved in the church and "growing in my faith", this incident featured prominently in my personal witness to fellow – as well as would-be – "born-again Christians" for the next twenty-five years.

One of my secondary school friends was a third-generation German immigrant. He was also a hostel resident, as his parents lived in Pretoria, like mine. My friend's father was a civil engineer and a part-time farmer in the Brits region. He grew a type of wild plant on his farm, the roots of which he sold to a German pharmaceutical company based in Hessen, Germany. At some point in our matric year, during a visit to my friend on the farm, I met Mr Augustin, the president of this German company, visiting his supplier in South Africa. Two years later, towards the end of my first year at university, I was informed that my friend and I had been invited to visit the Augustin family in Germany over the Christmas holidays. I then learned that Herr Augustin was so impressed with these two schoolboys that day on the farm, running barefoot and swimming naked in the river, that the invitation was already extended at the time, two years before. However, my friend's father had waited a while before deciding it was appropriate for his son to accept the invitation. My mother borrowed the R300 for my ticket to Germany from a family friend and paid it back over two years. My friend and I left for a three-week holiday in Europe, courtesy of the Augustin family. Our host, Herr Augustin, was a wealthy man and, as well as the house in Kassel, Germany, also owned a holiday house and holiday apartment in the picturesque tourist and ski resort of Seefeld in Tirol, Austria. We stayed with the Augustin family in Kassel for the first week but then travelled with them to Austria for their two-week Christmas break. My friend and I had the apartment – at the foothills of the Alps overlooking the ski slopes – to ourselves for two weeks over Christmas and New Year, all expenses paid. Fairytale stuff and my first exposure to, and experience of, German people and the Catholic Church in Europe.

We spent most of the time with the Augustin family and met many of their friends during our stay. From these people, I learned that none of them was a believer and that only older people and tourists visited the churches. Even so, there were churches everywhere, big and small, and all were exceptionally well maintained. I initially thought this to be a German good-housekeeping thing, but when I toured through Europe three years later with a backpack on a five-dollars-a-day budget, I experienced the same in France, Belgium, Spain and other European countries. Even though it was hard to find a believer, the culture of Christianity was alive and well in Europe, and the influence of the Catholic Church was strong and visible. Even in all of Bavaria where I live today, you will not find a shop open on a Sunday or any of the many religious holidays in the south of Germany. If you mow your lawn on a Sunday, there is a good chance that your neighbours will call the police. Not because they are religious, but because Germans generally follow the rules, and it makes no difference whether the church or the devil instigated the rule. It was, of course, not the devil that initiated these rules, but the church. We will return to this in the next chapter and explore the alliance between state and church in more detail.

When my hosts learned I was religious, they immediately offered to take us to the Catholic Eucharist. I was curious, so we went, and I found it officious and ritualistic but absorbing. Even though my Protestant background made me believe that all the symbols and rituals of the Catholics were false and idol worship, I was fascinated by the serenity I experienced inside their churches. I was also impressed with the beautiful architecture and the splendour of the paintings and sculptures. Either way, religion took a back seat during this trip. There were more imminent and essential things to discover and learn for a twenty-year-old Afrikaner on his first overseas visit in such dream-like circumstances.

Those three weeks in Germany and Austria were an exceptional experience from all points of view, and I came home with fond memories and a good feeling about German people, which also lasted a lifetime.

3

In my early adult years

After matric (Grade Twelve), I had to do nine months of compulsory military training. After initially being posted to the Administration Staff Division in Voortrekkerhoogte, Pretoria, I volunteered to join the Parabats and eventually spent a whole year – 1970 – in the army at One Parachute Battalion, Tempe, in Bloemfontein. I enjoyed my year in the army. It appealed to my sense of order and discipline. I think that volunteering for and completing this particular unit's substantial physical and mental programme also confirmed my tendency to test boundaries in seeking fulfilment.

Thinking back, I would say I was comparatively active in living my faith during my year in the army. One "struggle-with-the-flesh" I had, confirmed this: masturbation. In those days, masturbation was a particularly shocking sin. It could even make you blind! I made a pact with God: If he would help me get my Parabat wings, I would not masturbate for that whole year. I can remember trying really hard and praying a lot about this. Even so, I could not keep my part of the deal. But he did. I did not give it a second thought then, but reflected on it many years later when I was actively involved in seeking God's intervention in the lives of people and situations through prayer. We will return to this point in Chapter 5. But, as a tail to this story, allow me to add a humorous quote from Christopher Hitchens in his best-seller, *God is Not Great*,[2] when he says:

> ... *men produce infinitely more seminal fluid than is required to build a human family, and are tortured – not completely unpleasantly – by the urgent need to spread it all over the place or otherwise get rid of it. (Religions have needlessly added to the torture by condemning various simple means of relieving this presumably "designed" pressure.)*

Throughout my school career and as far back as I can remember, I wanted to become a medical doctor. However, during my year in the army, I realised that this dream would not come true as there was no money available to go to university. My mother applied for all possible bursaries available at the time, but bursaries for medical students were few and far between and only for the top students, and I wasn't one of them. However, due to her tireless efforts, I received a bursary from South African Railways & Harbours to study Civil Engineering. In the 1960s and 1970s, the country's road, rail and dam infrastructure was greatly expanded. I had the impression that anyone who could add two and two together could qualify for a civil engineering bursary. I was reasonably good at science and maths, so I made the grade. I then spent five years at the University of Pretoria, most of the time in hostel residence. To a large extent, I kept up the faith and my church-going activity. I met my first wife at university, and we got married while I was still studying. We shared the same passion for church-going and religion. Her father was a quiet, humble and deeply religious man and impacted my young but blossoming faith journey.

Varsity life was a lot of fun, and I tried to make the most of it. I participated in almost every extracurricular activity. I wasn't good at anything but ready to participate in everything.

On the sports front, I played rugby, tennis, hockey and water polo. In the hostel, we played a lot of table tennis and bridge between lectures. I even participated in one of the annual Intervarsity clashes between Tuks and Wits (the University of the Witwatersrand in Johannesburg), playing bridge. My partner and I lost our match. I did not miss a "sokkie", a dance party organised between a male and female hostel. I did not shy away from consuming alcohol, seldom said no to another round and could drink as hard as any. In Maroela hostel, I once participated in a multi-athlon event, consisting of items including darts, table tennis, running five kilometres and downing a bottle of beer. That year, I won the event. After returning from my European trip with my school friend over Christmas 1971, I entertained my varsity friends with picture books and magazines of naked girls I smuggled into the country. In South Africa at the time, these books/magazines were Sodom and Gomorra stuff and strictly banned. Some years later, as my religious journey intensified, my guilt overcame my desire to have a peek at these now and then, and I burned them all.

For me, there was also a very serious side to my university life. I had to pass every academic year to retain my bursary and renew the annual bank loans I needed to pay for everything, including the university's extracurricular fun life. I recall vividly how I sometimes studied through the night to the late morning hours with the only motivation not to disappoint the woman who created this opportunity and made it possible for me to be where I was.

The National Party had come into power in 1948, three years before my birth, and it took the nationalistic fervour of the Afrikaners to a new level. It replaced the United Party and ousted Field Marshall Jan Smuts (one of the world's most eminent political leaders) as prime minister. The Afrikaner language and culture were growing in leaps and bounds, and – in some instances – forcibly so. The Dutch Reformed Church was, except for a handful of smaller bilingual Andrew Murray congregations, all-Afrikaans. It was the biggest of the three Afrikaans-speaking reformed churches, which were also called the "Drie Afrikaanse Gereformeerde Suster Kerke" (the other two being the "Gereformeerde Kerk" and the "Hervormde Kerk"). The total membership of the mainstream Afrikaner churches at the time accounted for around two million of a (white) voting public of five million. It is easy to see how the Afrikaner churches' leadership would have a definitive influence on the politics of the day. Also, most of the leading figures in the Afrikaner church hierarchy were members of the Afrikaner Broederbond, which – among other things – served as a think tank to promote Afrikaner language and culture. Religion has traditionally been a powerful driver of Afrikaner culture. This is not surprising, as a recent DNA analysis of white Afrikaner ancestry showed the relation to be around 35% Dutch, 31% German and 20% French.[3] Most of the French settlers were from Huguenot stock, and a large proportion of the rest were also Protestants fleeing the Inquisition in Europe.

It took me a lifetime to learn that state and religion are two sides of the same coin and the most mutually beneficial bed-mates possible. I discovered that the state, not only in South Africa but worldwide and from time immemorial, has always been the senior partner in this alliance, manipulating and exploiting the gullibility of the church-going masses to move its political agenda forward. Religion has always been in the service of political hegemony. I want to share two examples:

- By chance, I saw part of an exceptional church service held in Washington in 2003 to show support for the decision of George W Bush to go to war with Iraq. I cannot remember all the details, but what I clearly remember is that all the former presidents of the United States – both Republicans and Democrats – still alive at the time, were in attendance. Many other high-ranking government officials were also there, including, as far as I can recall, the then Secretary of

State, Colin Powell, and the Secretary of Defense, Donald Rumsfeld. Very hard to believe that these eminent political heavyweights all belonged to the same congregation and were in attendance as part of their weekly devotional routine when this particular service was broadcast all over America, at this crucial point in time. It was a conspicuous and prominent rallying call to make the biggest possible impression on the American people to accept and support the political decision to go to war. From the pulpit, much ado was made of the righteousness of the imminent war, protecting the interests of the USA even outside of its borders, and to rid the world of the evil embodied by Saddam Hussein. It was evident that with this church service, the organised "body of Christ" in America had put its rubber stamp on the invasion of and war in Iraq.

- I saw in the headlines and then followed up and read about another church service in Moscow, early in 2020. Patriarch Kirill, the head of the Russian Orthodox Church, led the service, and prominently in attendance was President Vladimir Putin. The Russian Orthodox Church has regained its influence under President Putin. When Putin became president of Russia in 2000, he inherited the remains of a communist-atheist imperial state. After the 1917 revolution, the Bolsheviks and then the state apparatchik of the Soviet Communist Party managed to suppress religion for a long time. Still, it had remained latent, and Putin had recognised the power he could unlock by bringing the church back into his political fold. He often invokes the Russian Orthodox Church in his public speeches, giving the church a more prominent place in Russian political life. Patriarch Kirill, the seventy-two-year-old head of the church, is an avid supporter of the Russian leader, once calling his rule a "miracle of God",[4] and openly criticised Putin's opponents. The relationship, of course, is reciprocal as it always is, as the Kremlin spent 45 million USD the previous year restoring a residence for the Patriarch, if and when he visits St Petersburg. It seemed as if the primary purpose of this service in Moscow was to endorse the newly promulgated constitution devised by Putin, allowing him, among other things, to run for re-election an undetermined number of times.

During the last eleven years (2006 to 2016) of my corporate business life, my primary function was new business development in eastern Europe, focusing on Russia, Ukraine, and Kazakhstan. I spent a lot of time there, especially in Russia, and developed friendships and learned something about this vast country and its people. Contrary to popular belief and a large dose of ignorance in the Western world, Russian people have always been religious. And they are Christians, following the Eastern Orthodox doctrines and liturgy, as the Greeks do. It seems that the more people suffer in life, physically, socially and financially, the more they reach out to anchors, and religion has proved to be a very useful anchor. Russian people have, through millennia, been long-suffering, not only under the rule of foreign powers but also under their Tzar monarchies and even more acutely under the despotic rule of Josef Stalin.

In 988, after a visit to Constantinople (modern-day Istanbul), at the time the centre of the Christian Byzantine Empire, Vladimir I of Russia established a political alliance with Basil II of the Byzantine Empire by marrying the emperor's sister Anna. Vladimir I then converted to Christianity, was baptised and brought the Christian Eastern Orthodox faith to Russia. Legend has it, that upon his return to the capital Kyiv (the capital of modern-day Ukraine), he gathered all the citizens on the Dnieper River banks and had them baptised. The year 988 is considered the official date of the baptism of Russia.[5] Russia became a metropolis of the Patriarchate of Constantinople, and Vladimir I demolished all pagan temples and idols and built the first stone church in Russia.

President Vladimir Putin has successfully tapped into the underlying religiosity of the Russian masses. Since he came into power, many in the West have accused him of transforming Russia back into a military and imperial power with global ambitions. That is certainly part of it, but it may also have a lot to do with the Russian people's millennia-old fear of being invaded by foreign powers. The Vikings ruled medieval Russia, called Kievan Rus at the time, for 400 years before the Tartar Mongols took over and ruled over the Russians for another 250 years, up to the end of the fifteenth century. Russia has vast and open borders and is paranoid about its border security. Besides, the disintegration of the Soviet Union at the end of the 1980s, described by Putin as the biggest geopolitical catastrophe of the century, has led western powers – through NATO – to mobilise many of the former Soviet republics around Russia, despite having promised not to take military advantage of the crumbling Soviet Union.

When Ukraine applied for NATO membership, Putin drew a line in the sand and, according to western media, "invaded" Crimea. It is undoubtedly correct to call it an "invasion", technically and legally, from an international law perspective. Still, there is a very long history behind this, which is ignored by the West. Crimea became part of the Russian empire in 1783. In 1954, to mark the 300th anniversary of Ukraine's merger with the Russian empire, but more probably because of his strong personal ties to Ukraine, Nikita Khrushchev gave Crimea as a "gift" to Ukraine. He could not have imagined, in his wildest dreams, that the Soviet Union would be gone less than forty years later. The fact of the matter is that, today, only 16% of the population in Crimea is Ukrainian and nearly 70% Russian, and it is my opinion that more than 95% would rather be part of Russia than part of Ukraine. And the Black Sea naval fleet of Russia is based in Sevastopol, Crimea.

Putin has set himself up as a defender of traditional morality

– for instance, by opposing homosexuality, penalising divorce, and supporting the "traditional family". He has cleverly cast himself as a belligerent in the culture war. In doing so, Putin is even appealing to some conservatives in America who have grown sceptical of the liberal democratic tradition inherited from the European Enlightenment, which they believe contains the seeds of America's spiritual and cultural demise. One should not wonder why it was, in 2016, that the Russians preferred Donald Trump in the White House. The largest part of Donald Trump's voter base was middle-class Americans at home in the so-called Bible belt, where conservative nationalism and evangelical religious fervour rule.

An American friend recently mentioned, tongue in cheek, that Democrats refer to the vast tract of land between the east and west coasts of America as a desert of ignorance, which modern liberal people only want to fly over but never set foot in. The Christian Right in America is overwhelmingly Protestant Evangelical, and their ranks are of late boosted by traditionally Catholic Latino Americans converting to Protestantism. The trend is exponential, and I quote from an article in the *New York Times*:[6]

> *In Latin America, Christianity used to be associated with Roman Catholicism. The church held a near-monopoly on religion until the 1980s. The only challenge to Catholicism was anticlericalism and atheism. There has never been another religion. Until now.*
>
> *Evangelicals today account for almost 20% of Latin America's population, up from 3% three decades ago. In a few Central American countries, evangelicals are near majorities.*
>
> *This marriage of (evangelical) pastors and (political) parties is not a Latin American invention. It's been happening in the United States since the 1980s, as the Christian right gradually became arguably the most reliable constituency in the Republican Party. Even Donald Trump, who many see as the antithesis of biblical values, ran on an evangelical platform. He chose his running mate, Mike Pence, precisely for his staunch evangelicalism.*

During the 1960s and 1970s, there was a saying that "the Dutch Reformed Church is the South African government in prayer". However, as my commitment to the church grew in leaps and bounds during this time, I did not mind wearing this hat. I felt good to be part of the "bigger picture". This "bigger picture" was best described by the conviction of one of my best friends, namely that God deliberately planted the Europeans at the southern tip of Africa to bring the Christian message of good hope and eternal salvation to darkest Africa. And political clout would assist in achieving this outcome in the most efficient manner. At the time, I subscribed to this point of view. It was only many years later, as red lights started to flicker on my journey, that I became unsure of the merits of this "bigger picture".

I think I always had a sceptical mentality – the propensity to question and sometimes challenge points of view unsupported by reason or evidence. Maybe this is part of why I tend to push against boundary limits and be critical of authority when it seems not to enhance the living conditions in my environment and ignores the zeitgeist.

I recall being one of a handful of students in the early 1970s in our university residence who argued that apartheid was unfair to black people. Stating this today sounds like a whimsical statement or even a no-brainer, but believe me, in an all-white hostel at an all-white university in Pretoria in 1974, stating such a point of view was akin to claiming that I had just personally met the Antichrist and that he was not such a bad guy after all. 1974 was an election year in South Africa, and the university hostels invited representatives of the different political parties to address the students to share and explain their vision. The ruling party, the National Party (NP), was vulnerable on its right as the Herstigte Nasionale Party (HNP) splintered away in 1969. The latter targeted the fear of conservative Afrikaners that constitutional change was inevitable and that majority rule in a unitary state was a strong future possibility.

So, one good evening, we packed the community hall of Maroela university residence to listen to Mr Jaap Marais, the then deputy leader of the HNP. His main thrust was to explain and provide evidence of how the governing party, the National Party, was slowly but surely departing from their anchor vision of separate development for all the different ethnic groups in South Africa and, at the same time, to confirm how the HNP was ready and prepared to fulfil that original vision. Most of his evidence consisted of faded yellow newspaper cuttings from ten, twenty and more years before, showing what past prime ministers and other prominent National Party politicians had promised in the past. One of his main points was that, if elected to office, the HNP would implement the policy of separate development in self-governing homelands for each ethnic group and adhere to the crucial democratic principle of one-man-one-vote in each individual and separate homeland. For whites in the white homeland, such a system could only be possible if there were parity in the voting numbers. That meant that the number of black and white voters should be more or less equal and stay equal in the long term. Technically and in theory, it sounded like a good plan to maintain European culture and values for those who wanted to keep these. I just could not get my head around the practicalities of the plan, not to mention the fairness of such a system.

During question and answer time, I was brave enough to ask Mr Marais how the HNP hoped to achieve numerical parity in a homeland that covered more than 80% of the total land area of South Africa, given the demographics at the time. It was a good question, but I made the crucial mistake of getting carried away, and framed it too widely instead of keeping it short and concise. Afterwards, I remember how it seemed as if Mr Marais had a small, wicked smile on his lips as he started to answer me. He was an exceptional orator, and when he had finished with me, after ten minutes, even my friends applauded him. He wiped the floor with me without even attempting to answer the question. Mr Marais put paid to any latent ambitions I might ever have had to try my hand at politics.

In 1974, during my third year at university, I got a job as an exchange student in a university laboratory in the Netherlands for three weeks in December. I used this opportunity to travel through most of Europe for nearly three months, and did it on a budget of five dollars a day.

I think it was in London that I saw the film *The Exorcist* (starring Linda Blair), which at the time was banned in South Africa. My curiosity was such that I think I wanted to see the movie precisely for that reason. Later on, I read that this movie, loosely based on actual events, was one of the most profitable horror movies ever made. It is about a young girl starting to act strangely by levitating and speaking in tongues, and her worried mother seeking medical help, but the doctors cannot diagnose the problem. However, the local priest thinks that the girl is possessed by the devil and requests permission to perform an exorcism. The church hierarchy sends an expert to help with the difficult job. I was fascinated by the theme and bought the book by William Peter Blatty and smuggled it back home with me. Some years later, at a heightened stage of my religious journey, I became convinced that this book, strongly featuring Satan, should not appear on my bookshelf. I got rid of it, and more or less at the same time, I burned my soft porn magazines. To be honest, I must confess that I felt a greater sense of loss about the magazines than the book.

In a theatre in London, I also watched the rock opera *Jesus Christ Superstar*, with music by Andrew Lloyd Webber and lyrics by Tim Rice. You guessed it. At the time, *Jesus Christ Superstar* was banned in South Africa. I enjoyed it immensely. It was probably more because of the music than the plot, because the music was excellent, but the plot puzzled me a bit. It puzzled me because, as I understood it, Judas Iscariot was presented as a victim of circumstance. God the Father chose Judas to betray Jesus, leading to his crucifixion and death, and Judas only did what he was destined to do and believed was the right thing to do. It did not resonate with my sense of fairness. At the time, it provided a lot of food for thought. But I had only started my religious journey, and there was not much time or inclination for religious reflection for a twenty-three-year-old Afrikaner back-packing through Europe on his own in the exciting 1970s.

I was also fascinated by the movie *The Omen*, which was not banned – but rather featured – in South Africa. The plot is about a child, replaced at birth by his father, unbeknownst to his wife, after their biological child is stillborn. The hospital chaplain is aware of and involved in the deception, and all of this takes place in Rome, the city harbouring the Vatican – the epicentre of the Christian Catholic faith. The father (played by Gregory Peck) is an American diplomat conniving with a Catholic priest. A few years later, the diplomat becomes a powerful politician: the American ambassador to the United Kingdom. As the boy enters childhood, a series of mysterious events and violent deaths occur around the family, and they eventually learn that he is the prophesied Antichrist. The religious theme of good vs. evil (God vs. Satan) fascinates me, but the plot also hints at the relationship between politics and religion.

Another movie dealing with more or less the same theme, but without the political dimension, *Rosemary's Baby* (starring Mia Farrow), had a similar effect on me. It grabbed my attention, and I tried to read as much as I could find about the characters of Satan and the Antichrist and the number 666, which appears in the Revelation of Saint John. However, outside of the Bible, I could not find literature on these topics that made sense and appealed to me. Everything I found was too "fluffy" and "airy-fairy" to take seriously.

During my university years in the early 1970s, Dan Bosman

appeared on the scene in Pretoria and, in a short time, became a sensation as a faith healer. A girl friend and I attended one of his evangelical crusades in a local school hall near the university campus. We sat close to the stage and had a good view of the proceedings. After the introductions, reading from Scripture, praying, and some witnessing, the real action started. The details of all the miraculous healings he performed have faded over the years, but two incidents are stuck in my memory.

That evening he seemed to have focused on people with back problems. So he called for people with back problems and lined them up on stage. His take was that most people's back problems resulted from one leg being longer than the other. By squaring the length of the legs through prayer, the back problem would disappear over time.

So he lined up the volunteers, sitting on dining chairs in a neat row on stage, and attended to each individually. Each sat with a straight back on the dining chair, with outstretched legs in front. Dan took both heels of each person in his hands and showed "clearly" to all wide-eyed onlookers that there was as much as a two centimetre difference between the two legs' length.

He would then invoke the care and loving-kindness of the Lord through prayer and, in a loud voice, would appeal to the Almighty to intervene and sort out this design inefficiency of the legs. As he was praying, the shorter leg grew until it matched the length of the longer leg. Dan held both heels in his hands and made a very visual and vocal demonstration of the shorter leg's growth until the two legs matched up. He even asked some people if they could feel how the leg was growing, and I cannot remember anyone saying no. Unbelievable! Divine intervention!

To be honest, I was impressed with the first squaring of the legs, but red lights started flickering in my sceptic brain when we got to the fifth and sixth person. Later in life, I learned that this squaring-of-the-legs healing was popular among faith healers.

The final act was something to behold. After engaging with the audience and asking about severe impairment and suffering, an older woman stepped onto the stage, partly carried on, with crutches and all, by two able-bodied men. Her face was moulded in excruciating pain and discomfort. A long session of prayer followed. Not the type of praying you would do on your knees in the evening, seeking the face of God in serenity, humility and devotion. No: to say that it was deafening is an understatement. It was raising-the-dead loud.

I was often exposed to this kind of communication with God, where evangelicals gather in worship. *"In the name of Jesus"* was the call I heard dozens of times over the years. Mostly not in a calm, soft and devotional manner, but more in a scream with both syllables of "*Je-sus*" receiving megaphone attention.

Eventually, the old woman was asked to let go of one crutch and, after some more praying, the other. It all ended quite dramatically as there were tears all around, handclapping and praise to God as she walked off the stage, on her own, without the crutches or assistance.

This experience happened early in my religious journey. Even though I felt a bit uncomfortable about the whole event, I did not allow my sceptical nature to get the better of me. But I never again attended a Dan Bosman faith-healing crusade or any other faith-healing event.

Not entirely true because many years later, I succumbed and, this time, even agreed to be the patient. But hold on, and we will come back to this.

4

In my middle years

My first office was at Johannesburg central railway station, where I started my working career in January 1976. My wife and I lived in a bachelor flat in Hillbrow, and I walked three kilometres to the office every day. I had a five-year contract with the Railways to work back my bursary, but I decided to buy myself out of the contract after two years. Civil engineering and working for the Railways were not for me. I became a salesman selling technical products with a bigger salary and a company car. The bigger salary helped me pay back my obligation towards the Railways.

Even so, my father was hugely disappointed in my decision to leave the Railways. He could not get over it for years. I think the issue for him was two-fold: he could not understand how I could give up a degreed education to become a "traveller" (he seemed to want to spit when he said the word) and exchange a safe and secure long-term career in a reputable government organisation, for a risky sales career in a small and nobody-knows-and-cares-about American company. In fact, my father felt so strongly about me walking away from a strictly civil engineering career that he was shocked when I told him a couple of years later that I had enrolled for the Unisa Master of Business Leadership (MBL) degree. I think it is fair to say that my father did not understand and appreciate what an MBL was: to him, it was clear that I was throwing my career away. He never admitted it, but I suspect that many years later, he changed his opinion about that.

I did not have a good relationship with my father for most of the time. That, however, changed somewhat in my later years, as I became a husband and father myself, and learned more about his background and the challenges of his early environment and generation. It dawned on me that deep down, my father was a sensitive person, unsure of himself but with a huge heart, trying his best to hide this behind a masquerade of obstinacy and aggressive behaviour. During the last ten years of his life, I became fond of my father, and I hope that I honoured his legacy with my eulogy at his funeral. My father's formal education ended when he left school during his Standard Seven (Grade Nine) year and ran away from the school hostel to return home and work on the farm. My grandfather lost his farm towards the end of the great depression, and the family suffered from poverty.

Reflecting, I know today that my father was also a sceptic. He also never believed anything at face value, questioned everything, and – because of his curiosity – read a lot. Notwithstanding his limited education, he developed extensive general knowledge and a balanced insight into things. One evening I sat next to him on the carpet in our lounge, when, entirely out of the blue, he said to me:

"One day, the white man in this country will find himself in a fight for survival, which he will not win."

This was the mid-1960s; the National Party government seemed untouchable and apartheid well entrenched.

Years later, he questioned my view as, in my zeal, I was trying to educate everyone around me on religious matters. One of his questions was:

"How come that Jesus' own people, the Jews, who saw and experienced first-hand all his supernatural wonders, heard his words, saw his deeds, and on top of it all, his resurrection, did not believe in him?"

I remember my answer was that it is all very understandable because the Bible, in Mark 6:4, states that a prophet is not honoured in his own country and kin. My father never argued but asked these questions from time to time, and although I always had an answer, his questions and comments stayed with me.

We joined and became active members of the Irene congregation of the Dutch Reformed Church in Doornfontein, Johannesburg, during the two years we lived in Hillbrow. It was a unique congregation in the sense that most of its members resided in Hillbrow and Berea, both of which were infamous big-city neighbourhoods in Johannesburg and, at the time, by far the most cosmopolitan in South Africa.

I started reading the Bible with more intensity, and I took it seriously – the guidelines, the promises, everything. As a result, among other things, I started giving my "tenth". I clearly remember that in 1978 my gross salary was R750 per month, and I gave R75 to the church. One day, for some reason, I handed my R75 to the minister ("Dominee") himself, and he asked me if I was "a child of God", and I remember being honoured to say yes. In those days, the term "child of God" was still novel in Afrikaner church circles, and I was quite taken with the question. I kept up my tithing activity for many years, and later on, when I became a deacon, I realised that I was giving way more than the average.

We bought a house and moved to Kempton Park in 1978 and joined the Edleen congregation of the Dutch Reformed Church. It did not occur to me then, but reflecting on this many years later, I realised that, given our Afrikaner backgrounds and historical time frame, to immediately join the local church and get involved in the church structures was not even a point of consideration or discussion. It was the norm. Towards the end of the 1970s and throughout the 1980s, Afrikaners flocked to the church in higher numbers than ever before. It was the heyday of the Afrikaans-speaking reformed churches, and they had a considerable influence on the politics of the day, which were becoming increasingly tense.

I started my own business towards the end of 1984 and struggled financially for about three or four years before things started to pan out and then improved. My commitment to the Church and faith grew significantly stronger during this time of financial uncertainty and relative hardship. I started reading the Bible with even more passion and intensity, working through two Bibles and beginning the third one over the next fifteen years. I paged so often and made so many notes in the Bible, that some pages became unreadable. For about ten years during this time, I got up an hour earlier every morning to study the Bible, pray, and work through dozens of Biblecor courses. After being a deacon for a few years, I became an elder and was chosen as the head elder of the Edleen congregation when I was in my mid-thirties.

I would say that this started the second highlight of my "faith career". I was actively involved in the structures of the congregation. For five or six years, I "taught" final-year Sunday School students (catechism) before they would qualify to become full members of the church congregation during a very officious ceremony better known for the fancy new suits and dresses worn by the youngsters and parents alike. The handbooks used were the three essential Confessions of Faith of the Dutch Reformed Church. These were The Belgic Confession, The Heidelberg Catechism and The Canons of Dordt. Reflecting back, I can remember that there was always at least one pupil in every final-year class who would ask the difficult-to-answer questions on Biblical doctrine, and probably seldom got a satisfying answer.

One question that came up without exception every year dealt with the doctrine of predestination. The doctrine holds that God has chosen, before the foundation of the world, who will be saved and who will not. It emphasises God's power and sovereignty, and highlights the depravity of human nature and our complete dependence on God for salvation. I studied The Canons of Dordt in detail and read widely about John Calvin and his teachings on this theme, and at the time I thought I could explain the doctrine well, but I always felt that one or two pupils never bought it. I was also actively involved and mostly led three to four Bible study groups at any given time during the twenty-five years of my involvement in the Edleen congregation. I was honoured to join a weekly early-morning Bible study group consisting of the minister himself (my next-door neighbour) and two other senior elders, a small group of "senior" churchmen, who I thought would help me to reach the next level in my quest for spiritual maturity.

I did a course established by, and under the auspices, of The Centre for Continued Theological Education, Faculty of Theology, of the University of Pretoria. Dutch Reformed Church ministers studied at this faculty for seven years before they were allowed to enter the ministry and minister a "flock of Christ's sheep" in a congregation. It was a two-year course covering the structure, content and message of every one of the 66 books (and combinations of books) in the Bible. I was totally absorbed in this course, and – in a sense – it represented the highlight of my search for Jesus and my desire to follow in his footsteps. From this course, I learned that the unique message of the Bible could be summarised as follows:

God and humanity became alienated from each other as a result of Original Sin. God restores this relationship, unilaterally, by making humans new (rebirth of individuals). He does this through the birth, death and resurrection of His Son (also God) and the presence of the Holy Spirit (also God), who reveals these actions of God to us, guides us to accept them, convinces us of our sin, and helps us to confess our sins and surrender our lives to The Trinity God.

I took the Bible even more seriously, studied it even more intensely and wanted to make sense of the unique message of the Bible and its meaning in my life and my understanding of my part in the greater scheme of things.

In 1990 I was invited to a Gideons International meeting in Kempton Park and afterwards joined the Kempton Park Camp of the Gideons International. The Gideons International is strictly Protestant, and Roman Catholic church membership precludes one from entering the Gideons. I was elected President of the Camp and held the position for the maximum period of three consecutive years. I was a highly motivated, committed and enthusiastic Gideon for fifteen years and would describe the first ten to twelve years of my Gideon life as the third highlight of my "faith career". I participated in the funding and distribution of hundreds of thousands of Bibles to schools, hospitals and hotels in our region. Every year we placed a Bible in the hands of every Standard Six (Grade Eight) learner in South Africa. These were turbulent times in the townships around Johannesburg, and visiting the schools sometimes required police or army escorts. But we were doing the work of the Lord, and a quick prayer session before we entered the townships made everyone feel a little safer.

I was regularly invited to the monthly dinner meetings of other Gideon Camps to deliver a message and witness during a strictly twenty-minute time slot. Gideons International was/is a very disciplined organisation. We regularly visited all of the Protestant Evangelical churches in our area to give the congregations feedback on our activities in the community and receive a donation. During visits to some of the smaller evangelical groups, we were even allowed or asked by the local pastor to deliver the Sunday morning sermon. I had this honour more than once and felt good about it. I was fulfilling the mission of the Gideons: to save souls for Jesus. This was achieved by distributing His Word (free of charge), engaging in personal witness, explaining the way to eternal salvation and helping people to accept Jesus as Lord and Saviour.

One of the Bible study groups I established and led consisted of men of my age, but included members of other church denominations as well. There were personal friends in the group from "Die Hervormde Kerk" (very conservative Afrikaner orientated) as well as from the Apostolic Faith Mission, a Pentecostal Christian denomination in South Africa (founded in 1908 with the arrival of the first American missionaries to South Africa). At some stage, we discussed and worked through the Book of Job. As a result of my intense delving into the Bible, and this book, in particular, I came to believe that God had revealed to me a mathematical proof of the afterlife. Hold your horses; here is how I figured it out:

According to the Greek Old Testament, Job was the son of Zare, the son of Esau, Jacob's twin brother. Jacob was the Patriarch of the Israelites, and Esau was the progenitor of the Edomites. Job was the fifth generation from Abraham, the Patriarch of all three monotheistic religions, and may have lived around 1700 BCE. Job was a righteous man in the eyes of God, and God blessed him abundantly with worldly riches. According to the Bible, Satan dropped by and visited God after returning from a world tour. God boasted to Satan and asked if Satan had noticed Job's extraordinary faith and loyalty to God. Satan responded with a challenge by claiming that Job's devotion and loyalty to God hanged only on the blessings he received from God. The challenge was duly accepted, and God allowed Satan to subject Job to a series of horrendous sufferings to test and prove his enduring faith in God. Among other tribulations, Satan subsequently stripped Job of all his possessions, including killing all his children. (In those days, children, wives, concubines and slaves were part and parcel of a man's possessions).

Job passed the test after a prolonged period of suffering, and God rewarded Job magnanimously.

In the first chapter of Job (Job 1:1–3), the Bible tells us

exactly how wealthy Job was:

> In the land of Uz there lived a man whose name was Job. This man was blameless and upright; he feared God and shunned evil. He had seven sons and three daughters, and he owned seven thousand sheep, three thousand camels, five hundred yoke of oxen and five hundred donkeys, and had a large number of servants. He was the greatest man among all the people of the East.

In the final chapter of Job (Job 42:10–13), the Bible tells us that God rewarded Job for his enduring patience and loyalty by doubling all of his last possessions.

> After Job had prayed for his friends, the Lord restored his fortunes and gave him twice as much as he had before. All his brothers and sisters and everyone who had known him before came and ate with him in his house. They comforted and consoled him over all the trouble the Lord had brought on him, and each one gave him a piece of silver and a gold ring. The Lord

Figure 1 – Job was a very rich man before Satan intervened, but became twice as rich afterwards.

blessed the latter part of Job's life more than the former part. He had fourteen thousand sheep, six thousand camels, a thousand yoke of oxen and a thousand donkeys. And he also had seven sons and three daughters.

Here's the puzzle and the question:

The Bible clearly states that God doubled Job's possessions and gave him twice as much as he had before, and confirmed it by the numbers:

Job had seven thousand sheep
    God replaced them with fourteen thousand sheep

Job had three thousand camels
    God replaced them with six thousand camels

Job had five hundred yoke of oxen
    God replaced them with a thousand yoke of oxen

Job had five hundred donkeys
    God replaced them with a thousand donkeys

Job had seven sons and three daughters
    God replaced them with seven sons and three daughters

Why did God not double up on Job's children, as he said he would, and as he did on the rest of Job's possessions?

God did double up! The first seven sons and three daughters, killed by Satan's intervention on earth, are waiting in heaven.

The afterlife, or life after death, if you will, is not a theme of the Old Testament. Job and all his mates, from Adam to Malachi, did not know or believe in such a phenomenon. I rationalised it and thought of it as a hidden message (maybe one of many) that God hung out there for New Testament people to discover and be convinced that, at least, there is consistency between the two Testaments and a plan in place to back up God's New Testament promises. I shared my "revelation" with several congregation members, in some Bible study groups and at Gideon dinner meetings, and it was well received.

I believed it myself and, to this day, cannot find fault with the logic. However, my journey's experiences and the scientific evidence against an afterlife doctrine are too compelling. I expect someone will one day explain to me where the naivety lies in my interpretation.

5

In my later years

(when my faith started to falter)

There was no specific event or exact moment that triggered the doubt in my mind about my faith. It appeared unconsciously but grew gradually and steadily over a very long time.

I walked the Via Dolorosa in Jerusalem and visited all the holy sites of Christianity in Israel during a tour of "the holy land" in 1999. The trip was organised and led by a minister of the Dutch Reformed Church and had all the promises of a never-to-be-missed religious experience. Not for me. I came back with a feeling of disappointment. I did not experience the sacredness, holiness and elation, which most of the others experienced. One experience, though, gave me goose bumps; the bus came over the hill with Jerusalem below, and a baritone voice in the bus started singing the Afrikaans version of *The Holy City* (music and lyrics by Adams and Weatherly, 1892). Everybody joined in, including me. It was emotion on a grand scale, with tears everywhere. Thinking back, I was again amazed at the power of emotional self-indoctrination.

Our local Israeli tour guide was a retired teacher, obviously Jewish but secular, with an in-depth knowledge of Jerusalem's history and all three monotheistic religions. He answered all our questions factually – so much so that our tour leader at some stage took him aside and reminded him that he was guiding a Christian group and that his answers should reflect Biblical convictions and not his own. Incidentally, I heard from him for the first time that Jesus was not born in Bethlehem but almost certainly in Nazareth. At this time, I had not yet read scripture outside of the Bible. Although I was shocked, I was not overly surprised and took it on board as something to be investigated. At this time, there were already some uncomfortable and niggling thoughts swirling around in my mind about many of the "facts" and "eternal truths" in the Bible. The inconsistencies of Jesus' teachings, some of the factual contradictions in scripture, the scientific errors and some mythical stories seemed too far-fetched and naïve for modern intelligent people to take seriously. The mythical stories, I later discovered, mainly originated from much older pagan religious myths and were never intended to be viewed as factual but as metaphors. We will return to these topics.

From the pulpit, I heard, Sunday after Sunday and confirmed by the three Confessions of Faith of the Protestant Reformed Churches, that the Bible is the unerring, truthful and everlasting Word of God, given to us by God and proved to be from God. And that the Bible contains the will of God comprehensively. Also that the Bible is perfect and complete in all respects, and nothing should be added to it or taken from it. However, the deeper I delved into – and the more knowledge I gained about – the Bible, the more confused and uncomfortable I became with this rational view of the Bible. I am an engineer by profession, and because mysticism is largely lost on me, it never occurred to me that I could possibly consider some passages in the Bible as metaphors and try to imagine my way around some irrational issues. However, mysticism was never part of the Protestant Reformed view, and the doctrines and liturgy of the Dutch Reformed Church did not support it. So I grew up with this rational view of the Bible and a very personal God. I took the Bible and, therefore, all of the myriad promises in the Bible very seriously (as with tithing).

The Bible is full of God-given promises, and the vast majority of these promises relate to the lives of real people living here and now on earth. The few promises relating to the afterlife are vague, confusing and challenging to get one's head around. Moreover, most of the promises are of a physical, practical, and worldly nature: do this, and you and your progeny will live a life of abundance (harvests will overflow, land/children/sheep/goats will multiply greatly); do that, and you will live a joyful life and inherit the earth; do this and that, and you and your progeny will be blessed, will be called sons of God, will see God and will receive the reign of God on earth. If you have faith, you can achieve anything in the name of God: move mountains, walk on water, heal sick people, etc. I looked at all these promises and considered them in terms of the central and unique message of the Bible, and came to the logical conclusion:

If I accept and confess Jesus as my personal Lord and Saviour, give my life over to his Biblical guidance, and try my very best to follow in his footsteps, serve him, honour him, pray to and worship him, I will become a better/happier person, and if I can convince others in my sphere of influence to do the same then my family will become a better/happier family, my community will become a better/happier community, my nation will become a better/happier nation, and our whole western civilisation will become a better/happier civilisation and a shining example to the unbelieving and unhappy rest of the world, who do not (yet) share our experience of exquisite joy, wellbeing, compassion, inner peace and lives overflowing with happiness.

I believed this for a long time, tried to convince others of this, and did my bit to contribute to achieving this outcome.

My disillusionment was profound – it did not work!

It did not make me a better/happier person, nor my family,

nor my community, nor my country, nor the western world, which built its civilisation on Christian values.

Here's the thing, though: it worked for me. It always worked for me. But it did not work for so many other much better people than me. During my twenty-five years in the Edleen church congregation, I was intimately involved with the lives and the ups and downs of many congregation members and some Gideon brothers who ran into serious problems, such as financial, health, mental, trauma, etc. I prayed with many of these people, seriously seeking the face of God in the matters that weighed them and their families down (reminding God of his promises, as he challenges us to do in his Word). It was the experience I had with two such family cases in Edleen which shook the foundations of my trust in God to the core.

I would say that these experiences led to the first major turning point in my "faith career".

These families were, in my opinion, what the Bible calls "salt of the earth people" – humble, meek and mild, compassionate, tolerant, hard-working for the church and the benefit of other congregation members, always available to do the less exciting, most cumbersome, less rewarding, behind-the-scenes work, and always available when old, sick or needy people needed help. From the outside, these people were as obedient as people could be, childishly trusting and faithful followers of the doctrines of the church and, on the face of it, utterly dependant on God and his goodwill, love, care and stewardship of them. Yet, their lives and family lives disastrously fell apart! Not because of anything they did, but with hindsight, because of being unable to cope with the unfortunate and harsh realities life threw at them.

In one case, in middle age, the man could not cope with the pressures of his new promotion, eventually lost his job, could not deal with the resultant social trauma and financial stress and ended up in a mental hospital. He was later transferred to an old-age nursing home, much too early in his life, where he will most probably see out the rest of his days in desolation as his marriage also broke up.

In the second case, the daughter came out as being lesbian, and after severe stress, at home and in the community, she and her partner committed suicide. The family disintegrated, and the mother eventually hanged herself.

I will not even mention the effects on the rest of the family members in both cases.

None of the multitude of prayers or physical and mental support from myself and other members of the congregation seemed to have made any difference to the outcome in the lives of these families. I looked at them and thought to myself: where is the loving and caring God that they served for so long and with so much conviction and so desperately depended upon? How come that he reneged on his promises to simple people who could not take care of themselves but trusted him like children? Precisely as he commands in Matthew 18:3:

> *Truly I tell you, unless you change and become like little children, you will never enter the kingdom of heaven.*

It eventually came to me that these people trusted God with their lives, but lacked worldly common sense and application in conducting their lives to ensure survival. Like so many others, they did not possess the skills and the wherewithal to overcome the "unfair" challenges life presents. It dawned on me that in real life, God only helps those who help themselves.

This brings me back to the "pact" I made with God in the army in 1970, and I want to relate it to the general issue of the answering of prayers. I came to realise that I had all the skills and determination to get my Parabat wings, and God had no role in it. In the twenty-five years that I have devoted my life to Christ and have indulged in countless prayers for myself and others, I have generally experienced the outcome of prayers to be around 50/50. The 50% positive outcomes were all in favour of those people with positive life-surviving skills, and the 50% negative outcomes applied to the people without those skills.

I had to conclude: do not waste your time and energy on prayers, as it brings a false sense of security. The outcome (your fate if you want) is in your own hands. Deal with the issues that confront you in a practical, rational and worldly manner.

The second major turning point in my "faith career" had to do with the content in the Bible. I did a Biblecor course on Philippians and learned that the central message of Philippians 2 (an epistle of Saint Paul, the founder of Christianity) describes the "unbelievable" love God has for us, the crown of his creation. The father (God) sends his son (also God) to empty himself of his godly nature to become a servant (a mere mortal) and further humiliate himself to die as a mortal, on a cross like a common criminal. All because of his indescribable love for us. Add to this: God does not only love (his creation), but God is love (John 4:8,16). God is the essence of love. Love emanates from God. You then compare this with the aggressive behaviour of Jesus (John 2:15) when he, whip in hand, confronts the merchants, chasing their animals-for-sale (sacrificial animals for pilgrims and travellers from afar) out of the temple and turning over their tables, scattering their money in all directions. Hardly an act of indescribable love, compassion and tolerance. For me, this is and has been the worst incompatibility in terms of the unique message of the Bible. But there are others:

- Matthew 24:14 promises that Jesus will return to earth if and when all have heard of him. Really! And when will that happen, or rather, when was that most likely to have happened?

The most probable time would have been after the Roman Emperor Constantine legalised the Christian faith, and Emperor

Theodosius I (346-395) subsequently declared Christianity the Roman Empire's official religion. Christianity was the state religion of an empire that ruled the civilised world for a thousand years. The percentage of Christians in the world population must then certainly have been the highest of all time, and the reach of the gospel could not have been more encompassing. The advent of Islam, four centuries later, changed that metric forever, and the percentage kept shrinking ever since. Since the Enlightenment has started in Europe three hundred years ago, the growth of agnosticism further reduces the chances that all will hear about, let alone believe in, the human god's virgin birth and resurrection. It is simply just not going to happen!

- Jesus will return to earth as he departed, on the clouds, and every eye will observe him, as clearly promised in Revelation 1:7. Hard to swallow for my engineering brain. He would have to jump from one cloud to the next, manufacturing clouds where there are none, as he circumnavigates the fast-moving and rotating planet, or really take his time during his descent to give everyone a chance to view this unearthly spectacle. Although, to be fair, the earth was still stationary and flat when this promise was made.

A thought occurred to me recently as I read and learned more about "the cloud" that governs the movement and storage of most information available today. So, I am looking forward to hearing an innovative preacher claiming a revelation from God that the second coming of Christ "with the clouds", as promised in Revelation, in fact means that, upon his return, Jesus would present himself to all: not from a watery cloud in the sky, but through the internet!

- Having learned and understood the unique message of the Bible, I could not help but ask: Could this omnipotent, omniscient and all-loving God not have made a better plan?

A more straightforward, more elegant method of reconciling the crown of his creation with himself that could be understood and accepted by all? Instead of confusing everybody, causing friction within families and creating divisions between groups, communities, nations and civilisations, which led to unprecedented persecution, genocide, slaughter and murder of millions of people over millennia?

- Not to mention the reason why the Trinity God felt it necessary to reconcile his creation with himself – Original Sin. Humanity has to live a life of tribulations (separated from God on earth) because its primal parent had exercised its God-given gift of "free will" and consciously decided to disobey God in one instance. After that (from Adam onward), every single human being was created "sick" but ordered to be "well", with the moral justification that we were given "free will" to choose. How can a modern, intelligent and rational person get his head around this doctrine?

- When I started reading other religious literature, such as Islam, Hindu, Buddhist and ancient Greek philosophy, I realised how many other gods exist, and all of them have their followers. If I had been born in Saudi Arabia, the chances were 99% that I would have been a Sunni Muslim; in Iran, a Shi'ite Muslim or Zoroastrian; in India, a Hindu or Muslim; in China, a Buddhist or Taoist; etc. It makes a complete mockery of the doctrine of "free will" - to choose between right and wrong, good and evil, or to choose to believe in the sacrificial death of the son of the Trinity God or not. There is simply no such thing as "free will". You have no say or choice to determine your genes, sex or your place of birth. You do not even have a choice to decide on your next thought. Your next thought is determined by your senses and circumstances – what you see, hear, smell, taste or feel.

- Then there is the virgin birth. I learned that this miracle phenomenon was nothing new in religious history. Many gods were born of virgins, hundreds and even thousands of years before Jesus. These are legends, and like all legends, there are different versions, and details change as they are passed on as well as translated into different languages:

Romulus and Remus, twin founders of Rome, were born of the virgin Rhea Silvia fathered by the war god Mars. In ancient Egypt, the sun god Ra was born of a virgin mother, Net. The god Horus, protector and patron of the Pharoah, was the son of the virgin Isis. The god Perseus was born when the god Jupiter visited the virgin Danae as a shower of gold. Coatlícue caught a bundle of hummingbird feathers magically falling from the sky, put it safely under her breast and miraculously became pregnant with the Aztec creator and sun god Huitzilopochtli. The Eastern Roman god, Attis, was born of a virgin, Nana, on December 25. He even went on to be killed and was resurrected! A Mongol king's virgin daughter awoke one night and found herself bathed in a bright light, which caused her to give birth to Genghis Khan. In ancient Greece, Dionysus was the son of the virgin Semele fathered by the god Zeus. Persephone was the virgin mother of the Greek god Jason. And Plato's virgin mother, Perictione, was made pregnant by the Greek god Apollo.

No shortage of gods fornicating with human virgins over millennia!

- And this is not even mentioning the flat earth, movement of celestial bodies, and creation "truths" in the Bible.

I share the following (quite humorous) tale by the internationally acclaimed writer, commentator, professor and scholar of religions, Reza Aslan,[7] because it puts in perspective most if not all of the mythical stories in the Bible:

> *When the gods, instead of humans, did the work and bore the loads, dug the canals and cleared the channels, dredged the marshes and plowed the fields, they groaned amongst themselves and grumbled over the masses of excavated soil. The labor was heavy, the misery too much. So they set fire to their tools, set fire to their spades. And off they went, one and all, to the gate of the great god Enlil, the counselor of the gods.*
>
> *"We have to put a stop to the digging," they cried. "The load is excessive. It is killing us! The labor is heavy, the misery too much!"*
>
> *Enlil consulted Mami, midwife of the gods. "You are the womb-goddess," he said. "Create a mortal, that he may bear the yoke. Let humans bear the load of the gods."*
>
> *So Mami, with the help of the wise god Enki, mixed clay with blood and created seven males and seven females. She gave them picks and spades, and led them, two by two, down to earth to relieve the gods of their labor.*
>
> *Six hundred and six hundred years passed, and the earth became too wide and the people too numerous. The land was as noisy as a bellowing bull. And the gods grew restless at the racket.*
>
> *"The noise of mankind has become too much," Enlil snapped. "I am losing sleep."*
>
> *A divine assembly of the gods was convened, and there it was decided by all to make a great flood that would wipe humanity from the face of the earth so that the gods could finally be free of the clamor.*
>
> *Now, down on the earth, there was a pious man named Atrahasis, whose ear was open to his own god, Enki. He would speak with Enki, and Enki would speak with him.*
>
> *In a dream, Enki came to Atrahasis and made his voice heard. "Dismantle your house and build a boat," the wise god Enki warned. "Leave all your possessions and put aboard the seed of all living things. Draw out the boat that you will make on a circular plan. Let her length and breadth be equal. Make upper decks and lower decks."*
>
> *So Atrahasis built a boat and loaded it with the seed of all living things. He put on board his kith and kin. He put on board the birds flying*

in the heavens. He put on board cattle from the open country, wild beasts from the open country, wild animals from the steppes. Two by two they entered the boat. Then Atrahasis, too, entered the boat and shut the door.

When the first light of dawn appeared, a black cloud rose from the base of the sky. Everything light turned into darkness. The tempest arose like a battle force. Anzu, the storm god – the lion-headed eagle – tore at the sky with his talons.

Then the flood came. Like a wild ass screaming, the winds howled. The darkness was total; there was no sun. No man could see his fellow, no people could be distinguished from the sky. Even the gods were afraid of the deluge. They withdrew to heaven, where they cowered like dogs crouched by a wall.

For seven days and seven nights the torrent, the storm, the flood came on. The tempest overwhelmed the land. Bodies clogged the river like dragonflies. When the seventh day arrived, the storm, which had struggled like a woman in labor, blew itself out. The sea became calm and the flood-plain flat as a roof.

The boat came to rest atop Mount Nimush and Atrahasis exited. He released a dove. The dove came back, for no perching place was visible to it. He released a swallow. The swallow came back, for no perching place was visible to it. He released a raven. The raven did not come back. So Atrahasis and his kith and kin, and the birds of the heavens, and the cattle from the open country, and the wild beasts from the open country, and the wild animals from the steppes came out of the boat. And there he made a sacrifice of thanks to Enki his god.

But when Enlil smelled the sacrifice and saw the boat, he was furious. Once again, he called the divine assembly to order. "We, all of us, agreed together on an oath. No form of life should have escaped. How did any man survive the catastrophe?"

Enki, the wise, spoke. "I did it, in defiance of you! It was I who made sure life was preserved."

The gods were humbled by Enki's words. They wept and were filled with regret. Mami, the midwife of the gods, cried. "How could I have spoken such evil in the gods' assembly? I myself gave birth to them; they are my own people."

So Enlil and Enki came to a compromise. "Instead of imposing a flood, let a lion come up and diminish the people. Instead of imposing a flood, let a wolf come up and diminish the people. Instead of imposing a flood, let famine lessen the land. Let war and plague savage the population."

The divine compromise reached, Enki came down to the boat and took Atrahasis by the hand. He took his wife by the hand. He touched their foreheads and made a declaration.

"Henceforth, this man and this woman shall be as we gods are."

If the above ancient Sumerian epic of Atrahasis and the flood, composed more than four thousand years ago, sounds familiar to you, it should. You have heard and read the story of Noah and his Ark many times. You have probably read it to your children to calm them down and get them to wander off to dreamland so that you could continue your evening duties or watch television. Tales of a world-ending deluge that destroys all of humanity except for a fortunate few are among the oldest and most widely spread in history. Most scholars believe that

Figure 2 – Noah and his friends celebrating the rainbow, one of God's many promises to his creation.

the myth is based on an actual catastrophic flood some time in the distant past. Indigenous versions of a flood epic can be found in Egypt, Babylon, Greece, India, Europe, East Asia, North and South America and Australia. The reasons for the flood differ, depending on who is telling the story. Different settings, different gods, and different endings are reworked to reflect the storyteller's particular culture and religion.

In about 2002, I read *Quo Vadis*, a book by Dr Willie Marais, a well-known minister of the Dutch Reformed Church. To his credit, well-known is an understatement, as Dr Marais drew more churchgoers to his Pretoria East church on any given Sunday morning than the building could accommodate. He wrote fifty-four books, including one translated into thirty-two languages and sold worldwide. I was one of the hundreds of university students who frequented his services regularly because he was an exceptional preacher who seemed to know the Bible by heart as he seldom needed to read from it but quoted virtually everything he wanted to share. However, truth be told, I read three-quarters of *Quo Vadis* before putting it away because I could not stomach finishing it. His arguments were circumstantial and irrational, even for my – as yet – uninformed level of knowledge. Dr Marais was a proponent of Young Earth Creationism, and he applied pseudoscience arguments in his book to prove that God created the earth between 6,000 and 8,000 years ago and in six days! Fifteen years later, having absorbed dozens of books on evolutionary biology, evolutionary history, geology, physics, chemistry, palaeontology, etc., I tried again to read it but stopped halfway and finally decided it was total nonsense.

I want to return to my faith-healing storyline and admit to succumbing to another faith-healing spectacle.

I suffer from osteoarthritis. Apart from the painful and unsightly effect it has on the joints of my hands, in my case, it severely affects my shoulders. I had my first prosthesis (replacement) in my left shoulder in 2000 when I was forty-eight. I have had two subsequent replacements in the same shoulder, the last one a reverse total shoulder replacement. In a reverse total shoulder replacement, the surgeon removes the rounded head of the upper arm bone. Using screws and special tools, he then attaches a plastic socket to the remaining bone, facing upward. A part of the shoulder blade's socket is then removed and replaced with a chrome metal ball that fits into the plastic socket below. Completely the opposite of a normal shoulder joint. Technological magic! I also had a standard/regular replacement in my right shoulder. I undergo annual check-ups to monitor the regression in the shoulder bones, and the prognosis is that I will also receive a reverse total shoulder replacement in my right shoulder in the next two or three years. Suffice it to say: I have suffered quite a bit of pain over the years due to all of this.

It was just before the first replacement in 2000 that I was persuaded, very much against my will, to see a faith healer and have him pray for the pain and healing of my left shoulder. The only reason why I succumbed is that the faith healer was a young man in our congregation, and I knew him and his parents well. I did not have the heart to tell him outright that I was sceptical about his chances of improving my medical condition. So, here we were one evening in a room in his parents' house, and me sitting on an upright dinner table chair. His mother was present, but not his father, as I suspected that his father shared my scepticism about the proceedings that were to follow. I thought the lights in the room were slightly dimmed, most probably to create the right cosy and mystical atmosphere for the magic that was coming.

The young man started praying, walking around me and occasionally touching my left shoulder. Thinking back, I must say that as much as there was this inner resistance in me to being part of this spectacle, another part of me wanted it to be successful. And more so for the young man's benefit than for mine. A couple of years before, he had been captain of the secondary school's first rugby team, and he was a well-known and popular young man in the community. His parents were also notable members of the congregation, and his mother was very much involved in the church structures. However, he had dropped out of university and couldn't make it in the family business; it was clear he was a young man searching and trying to find his feet. Probably because of his mother's devotion to the church, he had also become active in the congregation and jumped to prominence as, for reasons unbeknownst to me, he had managed to acquire himself a reputation as a faith healer, especially among the younger people.

Because part of me wanted it to work, I knew that for any remote chance of success whatsoever, from a psychological point of view, I at least had to cooperate. So, at some advanced stage of the proceedings, I closed my eyes and focused on his appeals to Jesus. In fact, in addition to Jesus, he also invoked the Holy Spirit quite frequently.

I had noticed this trend growing steadily in the Dutch Reformed Church at the time. The mainstream churches in South Africa had started losing membership to the more charismatic Apostolic Faith Mission and to other non-denominational churches, which had, among other things, put a much stronger emphasis on the person of the Holy Spirit. The Holy Spirit seemed to have been a more approachable part of the Trinity God than the unsavoury character of the father part. In this respect, I cannot help but quote Richard Dawkins from his book *The God Delusion*,[8] when, tongue in cheek, he says:

> *The God of the Old Testament is arguably the most unpleasant character in all fiction: jealous and proud of it; a petty, unjust, unforgiving control-freak; a vindictive, bloodthirsty ethnic cleanser; a misogynistic, homophobic, racist, infanticidal, genocidal, filicidal, pestilential, megalomaniacal, sadomasochistic, capriciously malevolent bully.*

The Holy Spirit certainly made for a more informal and joyful gathering of believers, accompanied by lively music, which resulted in more active and wholehearted participation in the church services. The competition for church membership was revving up, but it seemed the Dutch Reformed Church was up to the challenge and adapting to new trends. However, I recall many church council meetings during this time resulting in heated debates when the topic of music was addressed. The younger and liberal-minded members were up against the older and prudent, as the latter could not imagine any type of music, other than organ music, during the service. The devil was still quite active behind a guitar at the time.

Back to the healing.

So, me closing my eyes must have been a positive sign and a ray of hope to my young friend because the next moment, he shattered my attempt at meditation, shouting:

"Did you see it?"

"No, what?"

"I thought I saw a flash. Here, on your left side. Maybe the Holy Spirit. Did you not see it?"

"No, my eyes were closed. Sorry."

Soon after this, I think he ran out of steam, and I wanted to go home. He ended the praying session eloquently, but when he asked me if I felt any better, I said no, but maybe in a few days because these things probably take time. He agreed, I said thanks, and we shook hands.

I subsequently put my faith only in science and soon afterwards received my first shoulder prosthesis, which was successful.

Around 2003/2004, there was an explosion of hitherto unheard-of opinions and discussions in Afrikaans newspapers on "the existence of God". A growing number of people, including ministers of the "Drie Afrikaanse Gereformeerde Suster Kerke", were debating the existence of God – in the open! An unthinkable development for members of the Afrikaans church establishment. At the time, I was unaware that these discussions were, in parallel, also very prominently taking place in the new internet milieu in the Afrikaans portal LitNet. I soon took notice of a book with the arduous title "Die Omstrede God" ("The Contentious God"), which was a summarised bundle of most of the discussions that took place on LitNet, put together by Thomas Mollett, Erns Grundling and Etienne van Heerden. I felt drawn to these discussions because they reflected my doubts about the "truths" in the Bible. I bought this book and couldn't put it down, and read parts of it two or three times. Some of the contributors to these discussions subsequently broke ranks with the traditional Afrikaans Church establishment and founded an alternative movement called "Die Nuwe Hervorming Netwerk" (NHN) in 2004.

Many of the founding members were ministers of the Afrikaans Reformed Churches under Professor Izak Spangenberg's leadership, himself an ordained minister of the Dutch Reformed Church. At this point, I had stopped going to church and had effectively broken off my relationship with the Edleen congregation. I had also officially left The Gideons International. I attended a few of the first meetings of the NHN before the international company I worked for at the time offered me an ex-pat work assignment in Europe, and I relocated to Germany in January 2006. At these NHN meetings, I was pleasantly surprised to meet well-read, intelligent, courteous and feet-on-the-ground Afrikaners, most of whom shared my exact religious experience. And as far as I could observe, none of them had horns, a tail or a trident. Although not actively involved, I follow them on their website; and make a monthly donation to their cause to this day.

During my last couple of years with the Gideons, the punchline of my message during dinner meetings at Gideon camps, to which I was invited as a guest speaker, started to raise eyebrows. I could see it, and I could feel it. I could not help but express my conviction that: if your faith does not work for you, it is useless, and you may as well walk away from it. I had stated this two or three times as a conclusion to my message before it dawned on me that this is a no-no for Gideons. Reflecting, I realised that I was struggling to digest and make sense of my experience of living my faith. I had gone through a long and arduous process of immersing myself in the Word of God, trying my best to follow in Jesus' footsteps, getting involved and practising the doctrines of the Body of Christ; wanting to make a difference. But, after digesting the results, I had concluded that God is not supportive. He was absent. Maybe somewhere else?

Here's the thing. I did not say this to try to convince anyone to walk away from his or her beliefs. I wanted to put this critical issue on the table and challenge believers to think about the practicalities of being a born-again Christian who wants to make this world a better place. Think deeply about your perception of God's plan for your life and how to orient yourself in thought and behaviour to be in sync with God's plan for your life. If necessary: to contemplate, reflect on, even confront your doctrines' irreconcilables and make amendments to your insights. Once again, my take is that your religion, *the faith that you live*, must make a difference – otherwise, what's the use?

I guess it did not work because they did not like it, and I was the one walking away.

It was in 2005 as I was driving past the Hartbeespoort Dam on my way to visit my widow mother in Golden Harvest Retirement Village near Magaliesburg when the thought first crossed my mind: *Could it be that Jesus is not the son of God?* I was shocked momentarily and forced my thoughts in a different direction. But only for a short time. The more I mulled the thought around in my mind, the more comfortable I felt with it. Eventually, I could say it out loud. I then again realised what an incredibly powerful force indoctrination is to control minds and, therefore, people.

6

In my final years

(when my faith finally died)

In April 2004, I bought and read my first book on evolution, *Ape-Man: The Story of Human Evolution* by Robin MacKie.[9] At this point, I had not yet had my Damascus experience, i.e. my final conversion moment turning from being a committed born-again Christian to a hesitant and searching non-believer. That moment was still about a year away. Even so, I found the subject and the book to be exciting and absorbing stuff. I read parts of it repeatedly to allow the content to sink in and reflect on the information confronting me. Among other things, it became clear that the story of Adam and Eve and the talking snake was written as, and was always meant to be, a metaphor.

The book started with fossilised footprints discovered by the late Mary Leakey, the matriarch of a most remarkable fossil-hunting family, at Laetoli in northern Tanzania in 1976. Although Mary Leakey, who died in 1996, had refused to assign a species to the footprint-makers, today's consensus among palaeontologists is that the footprints were made by our ancestor species *Australopithecus afarensis* who lived in Africa between 3 and 4 million years ago. The footprints' close spacing shows that the people who left them had a short stride and probably had short legs. It was not until much later that early humans evolved longer legs, enabling them to walk farther and run faster. Longer legs helped them to become more adept at hunting and surviving predators.

Not exactly Brad Pitt and Angelina Jolie strolling down Malibu beach, but with footprints astonishingly similar to what we leave in the sand today. I learned that human beings share 98% of their DNA with chimpanzees, whilst chimpanzees share 97% of their DNA with gorillas. This means that chimpanzees

Figure 3 – An artist's impression of Adam and Eve, 3-4 million years ago, featuring a hominid couple making the famed Laetoli footprints.

are more closely related to humans than they are to gorillas. I learned that – to paraphrase the scientific evidence a little differently – about 6 million years ago, there was a mother ape with two daughters; the one daughter was the ancient grandmother of all chimpanzees, and the other daughter was the ancient grandmother of all human beings. It sounds like fairy-tale stuff to newcomers. Still, I can assure you, the more you read about this, also from different scientific perspectives, the more this "fairy-tale" world of evolution opens up a most fascinating, absorbing and compelling narrative.

Discovering history and evolution

My interest in evolution really took off in April 2017 when I bought a book from the Exclusive Books shop at OR Tambo Airport just before boarding the plane to then Port Elizabeth (now Gqeberha) and on to St Francis Bay. I was browsing through the bookstand, and our flight was already called when I saw the book and remembered clearly saying to my wife that I had to have this book. I grabbed it, put enough cash on the cashier's desk, ran out and started a most exciting and fascinating journey of discovery. The book's name was *Sapiens: A Brief History of Humankind* by the Israeli historian Yuval Noah Harari. In rapid succession, I read his following two books as well, *Homo Deus – A Brief History of Tomorrow* and *21 Lessons for the 21st Century*, before moving on to the likes of the evolutionary biologist, Stephen Jay Gould, and others.

In *Sapiens*, Yuval Harari sums up the history of everything as follows [my emphasis]:

> *About 13,5 billion years ago, matter, energy, time and space came into being in what is known as the Big Bang. The story of these fundamental features of our universe is called* physics.
>
> *About 300,000 years after their appearance, matter and energy started*

to coalesce into complex structures, called atoms, which then combined into molecules. The story of atoms, molecules and their interactions is called chemistry.

About 3,8 billion years ago, on a planet called Earth, certain molecules combined to form particularly large and intricate structures called organisms. The story of organisms is called biology.

About 70,000 years ago, organisms belonging to the species Homo sapiens started to form even more elaborate structures called cultures. The subsequent development of these human cultures is called history.

Three important revolutions shaped the course of history: the Cognitive Revolution *kick-started history about 70,000 years ago. The* Agricultural Revolution *sped it up about 12,000 years ago. The* Scientific Revolution, *which got underway only 500 years ago, may well end history and start something completely different.*

It seems fair to say that the cognitive revolution catapulted *Homo sapiens* to the top of the food chain. It led *Homo sapiens* to master language to a level of sophistication which had the most deterministic consequence and which had put *Homo sapiens* squarely in charge of further evolutionary trends – forever! However, I have learned that the word "forever" has no meaning when one considers the evolving universe which gave birth to us and everything else that exists. We will come back to this topic in the next chapter.

Language allowed *Homo sapiens*, as individuals and families, to cooperate in larger numbers and survive in larger groups than any other animal (or any other living organism) on the planet. This process happened over tens of thousands of years, and it happened on two levels: a physical level and a metaphysical level.

A comparative example of advanced language skills on the physical level would be as follows:

A monkey would yell to its comrades:
"Careful! Lion!"
... and they would scatter in all directions.

Homo sapiens would say:

"Be careful! I have just seen a lion tracking a herd of antelope near the bend in the river, moving toward our settlement. We must decide whether to evacuate our shelters or accumulate a band of men to chase away the lion and pursue the antelopes ourselves."

... and they would deliberate the best course of action.

Moreover, being able to cooperate more efficiently in larger numbers than any other species on the planet seems to have been the critical factor that led *Homo sapiens* to overcome their closest rivals, *Homo neanderthalensis* and *Homo erectus*, at the time. An interesting point to note is that although *Homo erectus*, as a species, survived for 2 million years compared to the 200,000-odd years of *Homo sapiens*, they never evolved past a stone-age level. Could it be because they had not mastered language to a level of sophistication comparable to *Homo sapiens*?

Homo erectus (Erectus) disappeared from the fossil records about 45,000 years ago, soon after *Homo sapiens* (Sapiens) crossed their paths. *Homo neanderthalensis* (Neanderthals) evolved in Europe about 400,000 years ago and disappeared from the fossil records around 30,000 years ago. Recent fossil evidence suggested that the first migrations of Sapiens from Africa to Europe may have been as early as 150,000 years ago, but they did not survive. The last migration of Sapiens (modern humans) was around 50,000 years ago, and they survived in Europe and went on to populate Asia, the Americas and Australia. Even though Neanderthals had slightly bigger brains than modern humans and were much better adapted to the colder European climate, they did not survive modern humans. Recent DNA research evidence has shown interbreeding between modern humans and Neanderthals (and also recently discovered Denisovans from Russia). The latter has contributed between 1% and 4% of DNA of modern humans of Eurasian descent. No evidence has been found, as yet, of any Neanderthal DNA in modern humans of African descent. This rings true, as not all modern humans have migrated out of Africa to have had contact with other human species evolving outside of Africa. This discovery has opened up a fascinating research field into modern humans' genetic diversity. Apart from the noticeable physiological differences (e.g. skin and hair colour), research is underway to discover more about cognitive differences between modern humans of Eurasian descent and modern humans of African descent.

The advantages that enhanced language skills would produce for Sapiens on the metaphysical level were more encompassing and far-reaching than the advantages produced on the physical level.

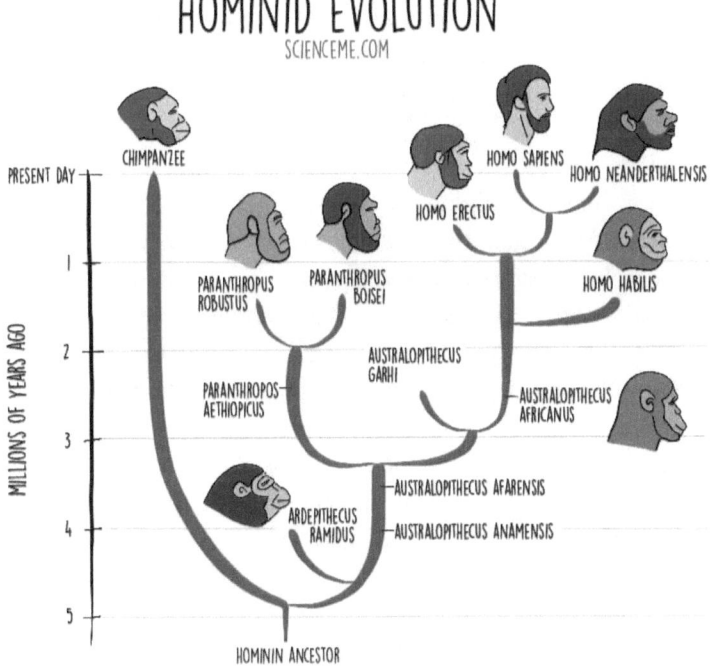

Figure 4 – This chart depicts one of the most likely routes by which Homo sapiens evolved.

Creating stories of all shapes and sizes and sharing these stories with their kin became a human thing. Storytelling is cumulative and progressive. Stories never die out but become collective learning as they are passed on and help to survive and advance. As far as we know, only Sapiens can talk about entire kinds of entities they have never seen, touched or smelled. Legends, myths and gods appeared for the first time with the cognitive revolution due to the advanced language proficiency of humans on the metaphysical level, i.e. storytelling. Later on, companies, nations and religions were some of the dominant stories developed, nurtured and told over and over again until millions bought into them. Then, as a result, they become a reality. According to Harari:

> ... *it's relatively easy to agree that only Homo sapiens can speak about things that do not really exist and believe six impossible things before breakfast. You could never convince a monkey to give you a banana by promising him limitless bananas after death in monkey heaven.*

Sapiens created fiction, and fictional stories gave Sapiens the unprecedented ability to cooperate flexibly in very large numbers. Ants and bees can also work together in huge numbers, but they can do so only in a very rigid manner and only with close relatives. Wolves and chimpanzees cooperate far more flexibly than ants, but can only do so with small numbers of other individuals they know intimately. Sapiens can cooperate in extremely flexible ways with countless numbers of strangers if they believe in the same story.

A comparative example of advanced language skills on the metaphysical level would be as follows:

A monkey would yell to its comrades:
"Careful! Lion!"
Homo sapiens would say:
"The lion is the guardian spirit of our tribe. Let us get

together regularly to pay homage to the lion, to show respect and discuss the ways of the lion."

The ability to verbalise fiction is the most unique feature of Sapiens' language, and arguably the most powerful tool ever devised to bind animals together in pursuing any single goal. This seems to be the dominant reason why Sapiens rule the world, whereas ants eat our leftovers, and chimps are locked up in zoos and research laboratories.

However, a critical point to note is that these stories change over time as insight and knowledge grow, and macro environments and behaviours change:

- Socrates (470–399 BCE) was a Greek philosopher and historian from Athens. He was sentenced to death after he was found guilty of impiety and corrupting Athens' youth. The real reason for his death sentence was that Socrates did not believe in blind faith and religion, but in reason and intellectual discourse. He was outspoken and sceptical of the pantheon of Greek gods worshipped by the masses and recognised by the state. Socrates also focused on ethical and moral behaviour, encouraged people to seek goodness and justice and said that happiness came from leading a virtuous life rather than material possessions. His ethos was so unacceptable in terms of the religious story of the time that he received the death penalty for his views. Yet today, Socrates is credited as the "Father of Western Philosophy".

- St Augustine of Hippo (354–430), one of the most eminent and influential Christian churchmen of all time, held that time did not exist before the creation (of Earth). He, among others, was instrumental in creating this story which held sway for a thousand years. When the European Enlightenment began around 300 years ago, countless intelligentsia made their voices known and questioned some of the Christian

Church's doctrines that had ruled the western world. The Church eventually had no choice, fell in line and changed its stance on this issue.

- The Italian philosopher, Giordano Bruno, was burned at the stake in 1600 when the Roman Inquisition declared him a heretic for claiming that our universe is infinite and many other solar systems exist. Today this is common knowledge, as even my grandchildren are informed about it.

- Galileo Galilei, an Italian astronomer, held that the earth orbits the sun and not the other way around, as was the conventional wisdom of the day. The Roman Inquisition also investigated him and in 1633 found him to be "vehemently suspect of heresy" since his view about the sun "explicitly contradicts in many places the sense of Holy Scripture".[10] Galileo was found guilty, forced to recant and sentenced to indefinite imprisonment. Because of his health, he spent the rest of his days under house arrest until his death at seventy-seven. This story has changed dramatically and is growing in leaps and bounds today as we learn more about our evolving universe.

- Only in 1951 did the Roman Catholic Church (the largest Christian denomination in the world), in a carefully worded statement from Pope Pius Xll, declare that the Big Bang theory and the Catholic conception of creation were compatible.[11] In essence, the Roman Catholic Church then concurred with the scientific evidence that the Big Bang was what Genesis 1:1 refers to as "the beginning of time" – 13,8 billion years ago and 9,3 billion years before Earth was "created". This view received support from Pope John Paul II in 1996 and again from Pope Francis in 2014. After a thirteen-year investigation, Pope John Paul II also reversed the Church's verdict on Galileo 359 years before, and in 1992 officially declared that Galileo was right. The spiritual descendant of Saint Peter and representative of God on Earth was finally correctly tuned in to heaven and got the message right.

Even some Protestant denominations today accept the Big Bang theory as compatible with the historical interpretation of the doctrine of creation. Notable support for this view comes from Dr Rowan Williams of the Church of England (former Archbishop of Canterbury, Archbishop of Wales and Bishop of Monmouth). Dr Williams also accepts the theory of evolution and acknowledges that modern humans descended from apes. However, adherents of Young Earth creationism, who advocate a literal interpretation of the Book of Genesis and believe Earth is around 6,000 years old, still reject the Big Bang theory.

Slowly but surely, as with evolution, the fictional stories created by Sapiens over thousands of years are ever-changing to reflect reality as science grows and ignorance and superstition abate incessantly.

Even though *Homo sapiens* has mastered language to a higher level of sophistication than any other animal on the planet, various lower levels of language abound among all living creatures and organisms all over nature.

A most fantastic example is the phenomenon going on right beneath our feet, known as the mycelium: a hidden communication and transportation grid, a collaboration between fungi, plants and bacteria. It is a vast neural network that binds the forest together, making it an intercommunicating, interacting and dynamic organism with the power to influence events even above ground and affect insects and animals. More than 90% of all the plants and trees on Earth are involved in this mutually beneficial relationship made possible by the mycelium. These days, the mycelium is aptly referred to as the *Wood Wide Web* (or Mycorrhizal, the Greek for roots and fungi). It is truly an ancient, subterranean World Wide Web, where messages are exchanged in electrochemical language, and nourishment and empathy are transmitted across species – even across the kingdoms of life.

- For trees and plants in a forest, the mycelium is their lifeline to one another. It makes the forest a living community. The extent of their root structure below ground is a great deal more significant than the parts above ground. The tips of their roots interdigitate with one another in the mycelium and create the infrastructure that allows them to interact, talk, and trade. And they do this through the fungi that grow in and around the roots. The fungi give the trees nutrients and, in return, receive sugars. When a tree is cut down in the forest, the neighbour trees are immediately informed of the situation. They reach out to the victim with their root tips and send life-saving sustenance – water, sugar and other nutrients – via the mycelium. This continuous drip from neighbouring trees can keep a stump alive for decades and even centuries.

It was not until the latter part of the 20th century that scientists first became aware of how acacia trees in South Africa communicate with one another – out of necessity. In all of nature, it is inevitable and common that one organism feeds on another organism. Insects and animals, among other life forms, feed on the leaves of acacia trees. It is also inevitable and expected that the victim organisms learn to defend themselves against the predator organisms. And evolution has taught acacia trees how to defend themselves against hungry giraffes – by equipping them with language. The fascinating fact is that the acacias are not only using one language – they are bilingual! They talk to each other in two languages, one above and one below ground. Let's say a group of giraffes loiter about a stand of acacia trees and start to nibble at the uppermost leaves of one of the trees. At the first twinge of a nibble, the tree responds with a three-fold action. Within minutes, it pumps toxic substances into its leaves to spoil the giraffe's meal. It then sends out a signal to the rest of its community by releasing an odour (ethylene gas) that the wind carries to nearby trees, warning them of trouble coming in the form of hungry giraffes. At the same time, it sends a chemical scream down to its roots and, via the mycelium, repeats the alarm to its neighbours:

"911! Trouble coming!"

From the suddenly unpleasant taste of the leaves, the giraffes know the acacia is aware of their presence and is actively alerting the other trees to the danger. The giraffes now move away from the stand of acacias, bypassing other nearby acacias to feed on trees much further away. It is not enough for a giraffe to move on to the next tree because it, too, now knows to produce the poison that can ruin a giraffe's meal. The giraffes have to travel some distance to find acacia trees that have yet

Figure 5 – Acacia trees defend themselves against giraffes that find their leaves delicious, by spoiling the flavour and warning other nearby acacias to do the same.

to hear the call to arms:

"Hungry giraffes are upon us!"

- Ann Druyan[12] believes that as far as we know, only one other species, other than humans, was ever able to create a symbolic language written in the physical laws of nature, i.e. mathematics and science. And this other species is bees. Having discovered a new source of food or potential housing, she (all bees except drones are females) will fly back to her hive and by employing a dance consisting of a myriad of complex movements, incorporating distance, time, wind direction and sun position, will give her hive sisters the exact coordinates of the find. The find could be kilometres away, and without fail, the swarm will fly straight to the location. Karl von Frisch, an Austrian scientist, studied this phenomenon in detail and named it the dance language of bees (*tanzsprache* in German). He could even express it in a mathematical equation, valid from hive to hive, from continent to continent and at any time of the year.

Amazing and unbelievable languages! But not the kind that elevates you to the top of the food chain.

Upwards of 95% of all species that ever existed on our "pale blue dot" (Earth, as endearingly described by Carl Sagan,[13] especially to those who today still believe that ours is a unique planet) are extinct. When a comet, asteroid or meteor (or a series of comets, as some astronomers believe, of late) hit Earth 65 million years ago and caused the mass extinction of the dinosaurs, it also eradicated more than 60% of all existing species on Earth. It seems there have been at least five natural mass extinctions since the Cambrian period started 500 million years ago. However, after each of these ecological disasters, fossil evidence suggests that life bounced back with even greater diversity than before. This means that the fact that species go extinct is very much historical reality and evolutionary normality and should not necessarily be frowned upon.

What should be frowned upon is the insensitive and inhumane manner in which Sapiens exploit other animals to satisfy their own needs and desires.

Growing up in South Africa as an Afrikaner baby boomer inevitably exposes you big-time to "braaing" carnivores and hunters. Most of my friends and their parents are meat-eaters and hunters of note. My father would not have considered it a meal if there was no meat on his plate. Braaivleis and hunting is an Afrikaner thing. Using sophisticated and expensive rifles, it is part of the annual agenda of most of the Afrikaner fraternity to go hunting and to kill as many animals as egos need massaging and wallets can afford.

Many summers ago, when my three children were still small, I wanted to show them how their father, at their age, used to shoot "bosduiwe" in Ficksburg. I took aim at a finch in our back garden, and when it fell dead on the ground: my children burst out crying; I was utterly nonplussed and thought the world must have changed.

A couple of years later, we spent a weekend with friends on their parents' farm, and I shot a rabbit. To this day, I can remember the feeling of sadness that came over me when I reached the dead animal and looked down at it. I never again willingly killed another animal in my life. I had close friends who hunted, and rubbed shoulders with real hunters – friends who have hunted elephants and buffalos and pay fortunes to have their pictures taken holding huge elephant tusks and buffalo horns in their hands, incredibly proud of their exceptional achievement and parading the "well-deserved" trophies to all and sundry.

Maybe I just never took to hunting, or perhaps it is just not in my genes. Even though my father liked his meat, he wasn't a hunter. He killed many snakes on his little farm near

Skeerpoort and once shot a baboon and hung it on a wooden cross just above the chicken pen. The snakes were all mambas, black and green, but he needed to create a safe space around the house. He shot the baboon because the troop was stealing and killing his chickens, and he figured that a dead, crucified baboon above the chicken pen would be a deterrent. Whatever you might expect, he was wrong about that because there was no reprieve from the baboons stealing his chickens. I guess the baboons have not yet reached the level of fictional storytelling to warn the rest of the tribe that seeing one of their species hanging dead on a wooden cross is a serious matter worth beholding.

Anyway, after I started to read Richard Dawkins and other scientists, thinkers and philosophers, and learned how life evolved from most basic beginnings and how all organisms are interconnected, I developed immense respect for life. Life in all

Figure 6 – Elvira and I visited the Taj Mahal in 2007.

forms and shapes.

I was fortunate to have had the opportunity to spend some free time in India after a three-day business conference in New Delhi in 2007. I visited several Hindu temples and even travelled to Agra to lay eyes on the magnificent Taj Mahal. This "crown of palaces" was built by Mughal emperor Shah Jahan as a mausoleum for his wife, Mumtaz Mahal, who died in childbirth. Construction started in 1632 and took twenty-two years to complete.

I was fascinated by this unique country and its people. Being from Africa, I have seen poverty and need in many shapes and sizes. Still, nothing compares to the extreme and utter deprivation permanently in your face when travelling in India. Yet, at the same time, I was struck by the high level of tolerance and respect evident in society, including indescribable respect for any living creature. I ascribed this respect for life to their Buddhist and Hindu cultures. Real as it is, I also came across a strong opinion about the reason behind this religious doctrine. It rings true because, as always, there is human motivation, primarily egocentric, behind every religious ideology. Christopher Hitchens verbalises it aptly when he says that the cow in India was:

> ... *cleverly denominated by the priests as "sacred" so that the poor ignorant people would not kill and eat their only capital during times of drought and famine.*

These days, I walk past domesticated animals like cows, pigs and chickens and look at them differently from how I did a decade ago. I have learned that we shared a common ancestor with them not so long ago. And that our relationship with them changed dramatically only about 12,000 years ago when we domesticated them during the agricultural revolution.

The transition to agriculture began around 10,000 BCE in east Asia or old Mesopotamia (the region between and around the Tigris and Euphrates rivers where present-day Iraq and parts of Iran, Turkey and Kuwait are) and down through the Levant into the lower Nile region, one of the most fertile stretches of land on Earth. However, researchers today believe agriculture also sprang up in Central America and China, independent of any influence from Middle Eastern farmers. Apart from fertile land being a vital factor in sustaining agriculture, Harari poses an interesting question and answer:

> *Why did agricultural revolutions erupt in the Middle East, China and Central America and not in Australia, Alaska and South Africa?*
> *The reason is simple: most species of plants and animals cannot be domesticated. Sapiens could dig up delicious truffles and hunt down woolly mammoths, but domesticating either species was out of the question. The fungi were far too elusive and the giant beasts too ferocious. Of the thousands of species that our ancestors hunted and gathered, only a few were suitable for farming and herding. These few species lived only in particular places ...*

Contrary to religious belief, God did not create Pekingese, Chihuahuas and poodles, but instead (if you want to believe that he did), created wild wolves, which over thousands of years were domesticated by humans to evolve into dogs. And today, some of them are even adorable and cuddly lap dogs. It seemed as if dogs were the first wild animals to be domesticated, but sheep were not far behind.

We do not know the details, but it is fascinating to read and contemplate how the domestication of different animals may have happened. Let us take sheep as an example, and the following is a likely scenario of how the process of domesticating sheep may have happened. I borrow the main change-moments in the process from Harari and present this historical piece of man-made evolution as follows:

At this point (about 12,000 years ago), our ancestors were nomads, with families and larger groups wandering from place to place, hunting and gathering food. Sheep were still wild and not easy to stalk and kill for an evening braai. The wild ancestor of the modern-day sheep was the beast to which we refer today as the Asiatic mouflon. The first step in the domestication process could have been to change how the herd was made up. Once a Sapiens group of wanderers found a mouflon herd, they would stick to them and initially hunted only the adult rams, the old and the sick. They would spare the fertile females and young lambs as much as was possible, allowing them to accumulate in numbers. Today, 21st-century business executives will call this long-term strategic thinking and sustainability.

The second step in the process would have been to lead or drive the herd of wild mouflon into a narrow gorge where they could proactively care for the flock and more effectively defend it against wolves, lions and rival *Homo sapiens* bands. Rival Sapiens bands? Even Adam and Eve suffered competition at the hands of jealous family members or, more probably, hungry members of other clans roaming the same region. Overpopulation of humans and reduced population of animal herds and vegetation during periods of drought were undoubtedly reasons why humans needed to become more efficient in food production. The domestication of certain species of fauna and flora also forestalled the need to travel great distances to find food.

Reza Aslan represents a different school of thought, which holds that the birth of agriculture (domestication of plants and animals) became necessary when Sapiens started building significant gathering places for worship. The recent discovery of the 100,000 m^2 site at Göbekli Tepe in southeastern Turkey, where the widely recognised first-ever religious temple complex was built 11,000 years ago, serves as a strong confirmation of Aslan's hypothesis. Many thousands of Sapiens worked on this site for dozens of years and needed to be fed, as hunting and gathering food would not have sufficed. They required a more efficient way of providing for the workers and their families.

Sheep were initially primarily raised for their meat and skins.

As time passed, they were also farmed for their milk and wool. According to experts on this subject, sheep survived by just dropping their wool and growing a new coat before Sapiens began harvesting their wool.

Finally, Sapiens began to make a more careful selection among the sheep, to tailor them (breed them) according to their specific needs. The most aggressive rams – those that showed the greatest resistance to human control – were slaughtered first. So too, were the skinniest and most inquisitive females. Contrary to biblical wisdom, shepherds are not – and never were – fond of sheep whose curiosity takes them far from the herd. The sheep became fatter, less curious and more submissive with each passing generation. The most aggressive and unruly lambs were first to the slaughter. The most submissive, most appealing lambs were allowed to live longer and procreate more. The result was a herd of domesticated and submissive sheep. God had created the first sheep.

But not the last. In July 1996, scientists at the Roslin Institute, University of Edinburgh, created the world's first animal cloned from an adult cell. Dolly the sheep was created in a laboratory, using an adult cell taken from one sheep to fertilise an egg from another. The fused cell was then implanted into a foster mother. It was a significant breakthrough in genetic engineering as researchers hoped it would enable new ways of treating debilitating diseases. Critics, however, are worried it has opened the door to human cloning. It is difficult to predict this long-term outcome, but it seems inevitable that cloning, possibly even creating life in some form or another in the future, is firmly in the hands of Sapiens.

I want to return to my earlier comment on the insensitive and inhumane manner in which Sapiens exploit other animals to satisfy our own needs and desires. I cannot express it better than Yuval Harari, who says:

As humans spread around the world, so did their domesticated animals.

Ten thousand years ago, not more than a few million sheep, cattle, goats, boars and chickens lived in local Afro-Asian niches. Today, the world contains about a billion sheep, a billion pigs, more than a billion cattle, and more than 25 billion chickens. And they are all over the globe. The domesticated chicken is the most widespread fowl ever. Following Homo sapiens, domesticated cattle, pigs and sheep are the second, third and fourth most widespread large mammals in the world. From a narrow evolutionary perspective, measuring success by the number of DNA copies, the Agricultural Revolution was a wonderful boon for chickens, cattle, pigs and sheep.

In this case, we are not referring to Darwinian evolution by natural selection but evolution by artificial selection and the selector being Sapiens. In addition, and unfortunately, this narrow evolutionary perspective is an unsatisfactory measure of success. It judges everything by the criteria of survival and reproduction, with no regard for individual suffering and happiness. The domestication of animals was founded on a series of brutal practices that only became crueller with the passing of the centuries.

The natural lifespan of wild chickens is about seven to twelve years, and of cattle about twenty to twenty-five years. In the wild, most chickens and cattle died long before that, but they still had a fair chance of living for a respectable number of years. In contrast, the vast majority of domesticated chickens and cattle are slaughtered at the age of between a few weeks and a few months, because this has always been the optimum slaughtering age from an economic perspective. (Why keep feeding a cock for three years if it has already reached its maximum weight after three months?)

Egg-laying hens, dairy cows and draught animals are sometimes allowed to live for many years. But the price is subjugation to a way of life utterly alien to their urges and desires. It's reasonable to assume, for example, that bulls prefer to spend their days wandering over open prairies in the company of other bulls and cows, rather than pulling carts and ploughshares under the yoke of a whip-wielding ape.

In order to turn bulls, horses, donkeys and camels into obedient draught animals, their natural instincts and social ties had to be broken, their aggression and sexuality contained, and their freedom of movement curtailed. Farmers developed techniques such as locking animals inside pens and cages, bridling them in harnesses and leashes, training them with whips and cattle prods, and mutilating them. The process of taming almost always involves the castration of males. This restrains male aggression and enables humans selectively to control the herd's procreation.

The domesticated bull, when castrated, becomes what we call an ox. An ox wastes away his life under the lash or in a narrow pen. He labours alone or in pairs in a way that suits neither his body nor his social and emotional needs. And when he can no longer pull the plough, he is slaughtered.

The dairy industry has its way of forcing animals to do its will. Cows, goats and sheep produce milk only after giving birth to calves, kids and lambs, and only as long as the youngsters are suckling. To continue a supply of animal milk, a farmer has to have calves, kids or lambs for suckling, but must prevent them from monopolising the milk. One common method throughout history was to simply slaughter the calves and kids shortly after birth, milk the mother for all she was worth, and then get her pregnant again. In many modern dairy farms, a milk cow usually lives for about five years before being slaughtered. During these five years, she is almost constantly pregnant, and is fertilised within 60 to 120 days after giving birth in order to preserve maximum milk production. Her calves are separated from her, shortly after birth. The females are reared to become the next generation of dairy cows, whereas the males are handed over to the care of the meat industry.

Immediately after birth the male calf is separated from its mother and locked inside a tiny cage not much bigger than the calf's own body. There the calf spends its entire life – about four months on average. It never leaves its cage, nor is it allowed to play with other calves or even walk – all so that its muscles will not grow strong. Soft muscles mean a soft and juicy steak. The first time the calf has a chance to walk, stretch its muscles and touch other calves is on its way to the slaughterhouse.

Allow me to summarise: Evolution is the driving force behind the existence of every living organism on this planet, and cattle, measured in evolutionary terms, represent one of the most successful animal species ever to exist. Ironically, at the same time, cattle are some of the most miserable animals ever to exist – because of us.

Foie gras is an expensive French and western-world delicacy produced from the fattened liver of a duck (or goose), force-fed for about three weeks just before it is slaughtered. Its mouth and throat are kept open, and corn, boiled in fat, is forced down its throat. The duck's fatty liver grows to many times its

Figure 7 – Foie gras production line.

normal size in a very short time. The duck is then slaughtered, and its liver becomes a gourmet meal on another animal's supper plate.

Beginnings and evolving life on Earth

Scientific evidence suggests that the first life on Earth appeared around 3,8 billion years ago. That is 700 million years after the earth was formed. Our star (the Sun), Earth, and the rest of our solar system's planets and moons formed following second- and third-generation Supernova explosions in our little corner of the universe, some 4,5 billion years ago. We will return to this theme in Chapter 7 when we consider the mechanisms God applied when he created the elements that our planet (and everything else in and on it, including us) consists of. For now, we will focus on *life*.

The first day we walked into the Grade Eight Biology class of Mr Robertson at Hoërskool Brits in January 1965, he challenged us with the following question and promise:

> *"If anyone can give me the definition of life, you will never need to attend this class again. I will allow you to sit in the room at the back reading comic books for the rest of the year."*

We tried our very best to find an answer, even from the "Dominee" (Dutch Reformed Church minister), considered at the time to have access to information not privy to ordinary human beings – but got nothing to satisfy Mr Robertson. It took me over fifty years to realise that we still do not have a satisfactory definition of life, even today.

Even so, it excites me to imagine and suggest that not only are we relatively close to an acceptable explanation of life, but that *Homo sapiens* may even be able to create life in the not-so-distant future. Even though the "not-so-distant future" could still be a long way off, it seems that if humankind wants to achieve this, it will have to hurry because scenarios on the table suggest that Sapiens will not survive another handful of centuries at the top of the food chain before something else takes over.

It also seems fair to deduce that the ability to create life may open up an unimaginable can of worms. Considering Sapiens' inherently selfish nature (probably an inevitable consequence of natural selection), coupled with today's unbridled greed and power, manifesting itself in extreme capitalism and growing neo-nationalism, it is realistic to fear that such a scientific breakthrough may hasten the end of Sapiens. And maybe even before artificial intelligence has the opportunity to take over the ruling elite's role at the top of the food chain.

In *The Selfish Gene*, Richard Dawkins[14] gives an account of the most likely scenario leading to the first life forms on Earth, 3,8 billion years ago. We do not know the exact makeup of the chemical raw materials on primitive Earth then. Still, scientists agree that among the plausible possibilities are hydrogen, oxygen, carbon dioxide, methane, ammonia and other simple organic gases. Hydrogen had since trickled away into space, but not before water was formed and the medium created for life to ensue. We know today that all of these gases are also present on the giant planet Jupiter in our solar system and throughout the universe.

Over many years, chemists have tried to imitate the chemical conditions of the young Earth in their laboratories. Stanley Miller and Harold Urey of the University of Chicago were among the first, in 1952, to mix these simple substances in a flask. They added energy in the form of ultraviolet light and electric sparks to simulate photons from the sun and primordial lightning. In all instances, after a short time of such treatment, a brownish broth resulted, containing different molecules – larger and more complex than the ones put in. In particular, it was found that some of these newly formed molecules were made up of amino acid molecules – the building blocks of proteins and, therefore, the building blocks of life. More recently, laboratory simulations have yielded organic substances called purines and pyrimidines, and these are the building blocks of the genetic molecule DNA itself.

According to Dawkins and others, the organic "primordial soup" which covered the young Earth at the time provided the ideal "nesting" environment for the first replicator molecule to be "born".

Ann Druyan represents another scientific school of thought, which holds that the ideal nesting environment for the first replicator molecule could have been the microscopic pores in the carbonate towers at the bottom of the ocean. These carbonate rocks were formed over tens of thousands of years from carbon dioxide and calcium carbonate, the same minerals that seashells and pearls are made of. The microscopic pores were ideal incubators for the organic molecules inside. There is no lightning or sunlight at the bottom of the ocean, so the energy needed to power the process came from the chemical reaction when the alkaline water entrapped within the rocks met with the ocean's acidic water. Complex molecules ensued with the potential to split and create copies of themselves, like DNA today. However, creating the building blocks of life is still not quite the same as creating life.

In summary, I will paraphrase the complicated biological explanation of the probable origin of life as follows:

At some point around 3,8 billion years ago, either in the primordial broth covering the surface of the earth or in the nooks and crannies of the deep ocean floor, *a particularly remarkable molecule formed*. It did not form by accident. It formed because natural elements in atomic and molecular form (e.g. CO_2, NH_3, CH_4, H_2O), brought together by natural forces and events (e.g. gravity, Supernovas, speed, light), interacted in natural chemical reactions, when natural energy (e.g. lightning, ultraviolet light, volcanic eruptions or heat seeping from the inner core of the earth) was added to the mix.

Today, biologists refer to this molecule as the *replicator* or *replicating molecule*. It may not necessarily have been the biggest or most complex molecule around, but it had the extraordinary property of creating a copy of itself. The first replication was an exceedingly improbable event, but given a 700-million-year timeline (the earth formed 4,5 billion years ago, and first life occurred around 3,8 billion years ago) and any number of favourable conditions, it was bound to have happened.

The problem here is the unfathomable timeline which is a mental obstacle for us. However, if one looks at it from a statistical perspective, it becomes a mathematical probability. If you buy tickets in the lotto for a week or two, your chances of winning are next to zero, but if you buy tickets in the lotto for 700 million years, you will very likely win several times. The replication may have happened independently more than once. Still, it may have occurred only once because once it has happened, the molecule's genetic makeup is established, and it (and further copies) will repeat the process. Once it had started, Darwinian evolution by natural selection took over and gave us the breathtaking and unbelievable diversity in living organisms we witness today. So majestic, that people ignorant of the process of evolution by natural selection ascribe the wonder world of diversity around us today to the involvement of a supernatural being.

Let's digress for a moment and have a high-level look at this incredible phenomenon that steers evolving life on Earth – evolution by natural selection.

We need to backtrack a little. The view commonly associated with Darwinian evolution by natural selection is the concept of survival of the fittest. Actually, it starts earlier. In *The Selfish Gene*, Richard Dawkins explains that survival of the fittest is a special case of a more general law, i.e. survival of the stable.

A stable thing is a collection of atoms that is permanent enough or common enough to deserve a name. For example, a unique collection of atoms, such as the Rock of Gibraltar, lasts long enough to be worthy of a name. A class of entities, such as raindrops, comes into existence at a sufficiently high rate to deserve a collective name, rain.

Things we see around us, rocks, oceans, galaxies, waves, are all stable patterns of atoms to a greater or lesser extent. A soap bubble is spherical because it is a stable configuration of a thin film filled with air. Salt crystals tend to be cubes because this is a stable way of packing sodium and chloride ions together. In the sun, the simplest atom of all, hydrogen, fuses to form helium atoms because, under the conditions that prevail in the centre of a star, the helium configuration is more stable (we will come back to this topic in the next chapter when we consider how God created all atoms in the universe). All things we see around us, rocks, rain, waves, oceans, galaxies, are stable patterns of atoms to a greater or lesser extent.

Sometimes when atoms meet, they link up together in chemical reactions to form larger structures called molecules. Some molecules are stable, and some are less stable. The stable ones will prevail, and the unstable ones will disappear over time. If a group of atoms in the presence of energy falls into a stable pattern, it will tend to stay that way. The earliest form of natural selection was simply selecting stable atomic structures and rejecting unstable ones. A water molecule (H_2O) consists of two hydrogens and one oxygen atom. The oxygen atom has six electrons but needs two more to complete its stable pattern, which is provided by linking up with two hydrogen atoms, each with one electron. Under the right temperature conditions, resultant of the earth being a specific distance from the sun, this atomic arrangement (H_2O) is extraordinarily stable. That is why we have oceans of water on earth. There is no mystery about this, no magic, and it is all explained by ordinary physics and chemical processes.

Back to the replicating molecule that made a copy of itself and started life on Earth: the thing about copying is that it is not without an occasional mistake, big or small. And the "defect" copy will also make a mistake at some future point. Accumulated mistakes over unfathomable timescales will create molecules with different attributes which procreate in divergent directions, resulting in diverse organisms. A copying error is not necessarily bad; it could be good for the molecule if it enhances its chances of survival in a changing environment.

As miscopyings were made and propagated, the primordial soup became filled with several varieties of replicating molecules; all descended from the original replicator. Unstable varieties died out, and the stable ones flourished. Environmental conditions on the young earth changed over time (as they still do today). Some varieties would have handled the changes better than others, lived longer and replicated more. Replicators of high longevity would become more numerous, and there would have been an "evolutionary trend" towards greater longevity in the population of molecules in the soup (or in the nooks and crannies of the deep ocean floor). Some varieties would have replicated faster than others, and their numbers would have increased. This would have started an "evolutionary trend" toward speed of replication.

A third characteristic that leads to increased numbers of the specific variety (species, if you will) is replication accuracy. The fewer mistakes a replicator species makes, the more numerous it will become. The moment it makes a copying mistake, it creates a new variant of replicating molecules.

The earth's size is finite, and the resources (atomic building blocks in the primordial soup to form replicators) were limited. The different varieties competed for scarce resources, and there was a struggle for existence among them. They did not know they were struggling; nor did they worry about it; the struggle was conducted without any hard feelings, indeed without feelings of any kind. But they were struggling as each variety wanted to live longer and have more children, and as the population increased, the resources decreased. The process of improvement was cumulative, in the sense that any miscopying that resulted in a higher level of stability or a new way of reducing the stability of rivals was automatically preserved and multiplied. According to Dawkins:

> *Ways of increasing stability and of decreasing rivals' stability became more elaborate and more efficient. Some of them may even have 'discovered' how to break up molecules of rival varieties chemically, and to use the building blocks so released for making their own copies. These proto-carnivores simultaneously obtained food and removed competing rivals. Other replicators perhaps discovered how to protect themselves, either chemically, or by building a physical wall of protein around themselves. This may have been how the first living cells appeared. Replicators began not merely to exist, but to construct for themselves containers, vehicles for their continued existence. The replicators that survived were the ones that built* survival machines *for themselves to live in. The first survival machines probably consisted of nothing more than a protective coat. But making a living got steadily harder as new rivals arose with better and more effective survival machines. Survival machines got bigger and more elaborate, and the process was cumulative and progressive.*

So, what happened to these ancient replicators 3,8 billion years on? Dawkins goes on to say:

> *They did not die out, for they are past masters of the survival arts. But do not look for them floating loose in the sea; they gave up that cavalier freedom long ago. Now they swarm in huge colonies, safe inside gigantic lumbering robots, sealed off from the outside world, communicating with it by tortuous indirect routes, manipulating it by remote control. They are in you and in me; they created us, body and mind; and their preservation is the ultimate rationale for our existence. They have come a long way, those replicators. Now they go by the name of genes, and we are their survival machines.*

As I am writing here, the SARS-CoV-2 strain of

the coronavirus is mutating and is causing havoc in South Africa, India and other parts of the world. It seems South Africa is currently in the middle of the third wave propagated by the so-called Delta variant of the SARS-CoV-2 virus (commonly referred to as Covid-19).

What is happening here is precisely what we have just covered. The Delta variant is the fourth identifiable variant of the original SARS-CoV-2 virus molecule. Like all other molecules in our body, virus molecules also replicate fast and furiously and are inevitably making copying mistakes. Some mistakes are good for the virus, and some are bad. The molecules resulting from the "bad" copying mistakes die out quickly, but the molecules resulting from the "good" copying mistakes extend the virus' life, helping it produce more progeny and expanding its gene pool. The molecules resulting from the "bad" mistakes are killed by our immune system and or vaccination. In contrast, the molecules resulting from the "good" mistakes overcome the soldier molecules of our immune system and vaccination, and make us sick or kill us. The truth, however, is that the virus has no intention of killing you. If it kills you, it and its mates will perish too. It wants to keep you alive as long as possible to spread its progeny as widely as possible. The virus is a living organism, and if ever there is a purpose in life – this is it!

By way of a practical example of evolution, let me share the fascinating story of how God created Samurai crabs, found in the Inland Sea in Japan, using a combination of artificial (human) selection and natural selection. I came across this story in *Cosmos*, the classic bestseller of Carl Sagan. The preceding legend goes like this:

> In the year 1185, the Emperor of Japan was a seven-year-old boy named Antoku. He was the nominal leader of a clan of samurai called the Heike, who were engaged in a long and bloody war with another samurai clan, the Genji. Each asserted a superior ancestral claim to the imperial throne. Their decisive naval encounter, with the Emperor on board ship, occurred at Danno-ura in the Japanese Inland Sea on April 24, 1185. The Heike were outnumbered, and outmaneuvered. Many were killed. The survivors, in massive numbers, threw themselves into the sea and drowned. The Lady Nii, grandmother of the Emperor, resolved that she and Antoku would not be captured by the enemy. What happened next is told in *The Tale of the Heike*:
>
> The Emperor was seven years old that year but looked much older. He was so lovely that he seemed to shed a brilliant radiance and his long, black hair hung loose far down his back. With a look of surprise and anxiety on his face he asked the Lady Nii, "Where are you taking me?"
>
> She turned to the youthful sovereign, with tears streaming down her cheeks, and ... comforted him, binding up his long hair in his dove-colored robe. Blinded with tears, the child sovereign put his beautiful, small hands together. He turned first to the East to say farewell to the god of Ise and then to the West to repeat the Nembutsu [a prayer to the Amida Buddha]. The Lady Nii took him tightly in her arms and with the words "In the depths of the ocean is our capitol," sank with him at last beneath the waves.
>
> The entire Heike battle fleet was destroyed. Only forty-three women survived. These ladies-in-waiting of the imperial court were forced to sell flowers and other favors to the fishermen near the scene of the battle. The Heike almost vanished from history. But a ragtag group of the former ladies-in-waiting and their offspring by the fisherfolk established a festival to commemorate the battle. It takes place on the twenty-fourth of April every year to this day. Fishermen who are the descendents [sic] of the Heike dress in hemp and black headgear and proceed to the Akama shrine which contains the mausoleum of the devoted Emperor. There they watch a play portraying the events that followed the Battle of Danno-ura. For

centuries after, people imagined that they could discern ghostly samurai armies vainly striving to bail the sea, to cleanse the blood and defeat and humiliation.

The fishermen say the Heike samurai wander the bottoms of the Inland Sea still – in the form of crabs. There are crabs to be found here with curious markings on their backs, patterns and indentations that disturbingly resemble the face of a samurai. When caught, these crabs are not eaten, but are returned to the sea in commemoration of the doleful events at Danno-ura.

How does it come about that the face of a warrior is incised on the carapace of a Heikea crab? The answer seems to be a combination of artificial (human) and natural selection over a very long time. Suppose that, by chance, one of this crab's distant ancestors arose with a pattern that resembled, even slightly, a human face. Even before the battle of Danno-ura, fishermen may have been reluctant to eat such a crab. In throwing it back, they set in motion an evolutionary process: If you are a crab and your carapace is ordinary, the humans will eat you. Your line will have fewer descendents. If your carapace looks a little like a face, they will throw you back. You will leave more descendents. Crabs had a substantial investment in the patterns on their carapaces. As the generations passed, of crabs and fishermen alike, the crabs with patterns that most resembled a samurai face survived preferentially until eventually, there was produced not just a human face, not just a Japanese face, but the visage of a fierce and scowling samurai.

Let me share another fascinating insight into storytelling and evolution, the two major themes that define us, *Homo sapiens*, and brought us to where we are today. Like all our organs, the brain has evolved, and increased in complexity and information content over millions of years. Our brain is the centre of us, the centre of our consciousness. Because the latter is still a bit of a puzzle, vast amounts of research, experimenting and postulating are deployed to understand more of the brain and its workings.

Between the 1960s and 1990s, the American neuroscientist Paul MacLean developed and proposed the Triune Brain Hypothesis theory. Even though some of his contemporaries were sceptical about his theory (not uncommon in science), it became widely popular, not least because the astronomer Carl Sagan adopted and gave credibility to it in his Pulitzer Prize-winning book, *The Dragons of Eden*.

MacLean's theory goes like this:

The brain evolved from the inside out and developed in successive stages. Deep inside is the oldest part, the brainstem, which conducts the essential biological functions of heartbeat and respiration. Capping the brainstem is the R-complex (reptile complex), the seat of aggression, ritual, territoriality and social hierarchy, which evolved hundreds of millions of years ago in our reptilian ancestors; and, as poignantly stated by Carl Sagan in *Cosmos*:

> *Deep inside the skull of every one of us, there is something like the brain of a crocodile.*

Capping the R-complex is the mammalian brain or limbic system, which evolved tens of millions of years ago in ancestors who were mammals but not yet primates. This part of the brain is the primary source of our moods, emotions, and concern and care for our young. And finally, on the outside, living in an uneasy truce with the two more primitive brains below, we find the cerebral cortex, which evolved millions of years ago in our primate ancestors. Comprising more than two-thirds of the brain mass, the cerebral cortex is the source of intuition and critical analysis. Here, we have ideas and inspirations, read and write, do mathematics and compose music. The cerebral cortex is the distinction of our species, the seat of our humanity. Civilisation is the product of the cerebral cortex. So, in terms of this hypothesis, brain evolution is an additive process: new layers of brain tissue emerge on top of old layers, leading to a tenuous but effective coexistence between the "old brains" and the "new brain."

To me, MacLean's story sounded feasible, and I wasn't alone. His model became part of the cultural zeitgeist, probably not least because it was a neuroanatomical cousin to Freud's tripartite view of the mind, with its warring superego, ego and id. It held sway for a few decades until it was recently finally debunked. Terrence Deacon, Ph.D., an expert on the evolution of human cognition at the University of California, Berkeley, submitted that MacLean's basic premise – his "hats on top of hats' view" that brain systems were added, layer upon layer, over the course of evolution – was mistaken. According to Deacon, as quoted by Peter Farley,[15] sufficient subsequent research has revealed that:

Adding on is almost certainly not the way the brain has evolved ... Instead, the same structures have become modified in different ways in different lineages.

Daniel Toker[16] wrote an article in *The Brain Scientist* where he says that humans are both extraordinary and unique because they are the only entity in the universe that has produced art, science, technology and civilisation. He continues to say:

But, our history of searching for how, precisely, we came to be exceptional has often led to bad science – and to popular acceptance of bad science. Nowhere is that clearer than in the hugely popular – and entirely wrong – theory called the Triune Brain Hypothesis.

Toker continues by pointing out:

The theory is wrong for a simple reason: our brains aren't fundamentally different from those of reptiles, or even from those of fish. Every mammal

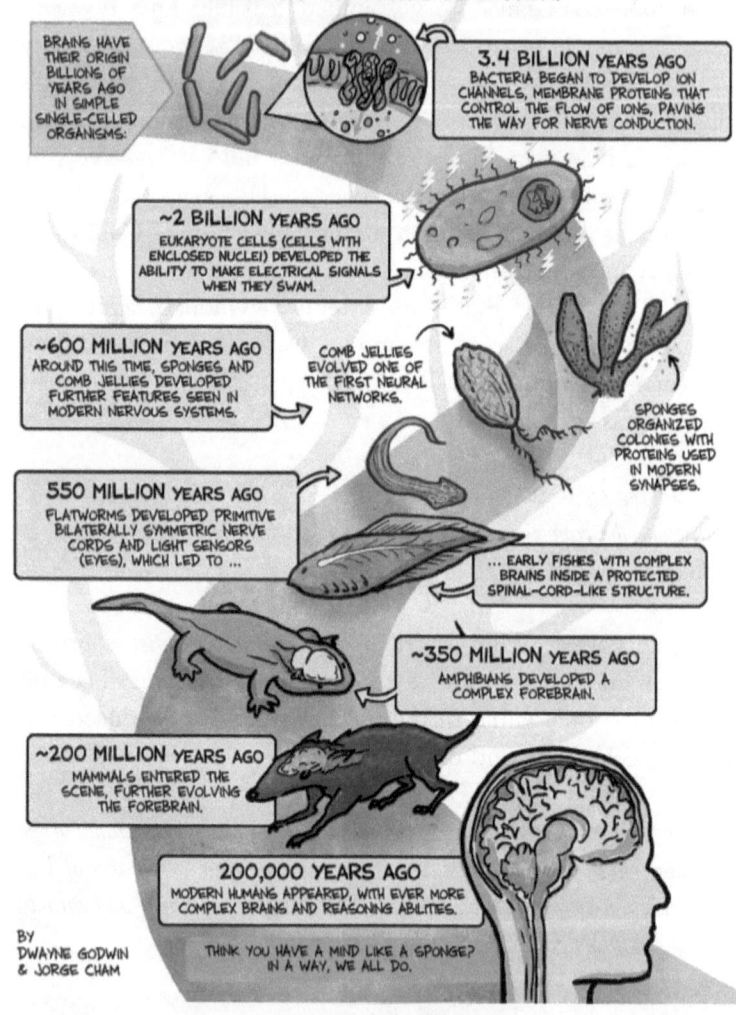

Figure 8 – How brain evolution actually works. New brain areas are not usually added on top of old ones, but instead are typically just modified versions of old structures. All vertebrates, from fish to humans, have the same general brain layout.

has a neocortex (not just the really intelligent ones), and all vertebrates, including reptiles, birds, amphibians, and fish, have analogues of a cortex.

In fact, the very idea that new brain structures emerge on top of old ones is fundamentally at odds with how evolution usually works: biological structures are typically just modified versions of older structures. For example, the mammalian neocortex isn't a completely new structure like MacLean thought it was, but instead is a modification of the repitilian [sic] cortex.

This is the incredible wonder of science: there are no eternal truths. New evidence and knowledge replace outdated ones, however sweet and sound the old ones appeared. Paul Maclean had a good story, and it held sway for three decades until new insights and scientific evidence finally debunked it.

All life on Earth can be traced back to a common single-celled ancestral species. Interestingly, for the first 3,3 billion years of life on Earth (i.e. after the first replicator did its thing), very little in terms of life-growth excitement occurred. It was only with what scientists call the Cambrian explosion, some 500 million years ago, that life started to grow leaves, trunks, arms, legs, eyes, gills and wings. All this happened after bacteria (cyanobacteria, or blue-green algae) ruled Earth for a large part of the preceding 3,3 thousand million years. The atmosphere of the young earth consisted mainly of carbon dioxide. Few, if any, organisms requiring oxygen for their metabolism could live in this environment. Fortunately for us, the metabolism of cyanobacteria (single-cell organisms) was such that it used carbon dioxide for energy-to-food synthesis and secreted oxygen as a waste product. This process is called photosynthesis. During this time, the bacteria increased the atmospheric oxygen, which varied from 10% to 35% over long periods and later settled at the current level of 21%. The increased level of oxygen in our atmosphere then led to the emergence of the ozone layer above the atmosphere. The ozone layer formed as a result of the action of the sun's ultraviolet radiation on the oxygen molecules in the atmosphere. This protective layer eventually made it possible for life to break out of the safety of the oceans and inhabit the land without being assaulted by the sun's deadly ultraviolet rays. God started to create land creatures, 500 million years ago.

After having evolved on land for millions of years and become what we today term mammals, some of these creatures found their way back to the oceans more than 50 million years ago. Whales and dolphins are the best-known creatures that have taken this route. They are still considered mammals today, as they still have lungs rather than gills, cannot breathe underwater, have to surface for oxygen, and give birth to their young. An interesting thought to entertain is, other influences being the same, that evolution by natural selection may reverse the evolutionary process for these creatures over the next few million years, turning whales and dolphins back into fish. Unless, of course, God decided that he made them mammals – and mammals they will remain. Through DNA sequencing, we know today that a cow is more closely related to a whale than it is to a horse.

So, for billions of years, life only oozed, but then around 500 million years ago, it literally started to swim, run, jump and fly. A vast variety of life forms (different species) evolved during the Cambrian explosion. About halfway through the Cambrian age, 240 million years ago, the dinosaurs rose to the top of the food chain and became the dominant species on Earth, ruling the daylight economy for nearly 200 million years. Our ancestors, the mammals, had to be content to be night-time dwellers among the other life forms. The dominance of the dinosaurs ensured that our mammalian ancestors remained no larger than a cat. When a catastrophic asteroid, meteor or comet – maybe a few comets, as some scientists are now arguing – finished off the dinosaurs 65 million years ago, mammals got the most crucial evolutionary opportunity they would ever have. They jumped on it and, utilising the earth's resources to their advantage, became the dominant life form on the planet. About 25 million years ago, apes started to evolve from their mammalian ancestry. Six million years ago, our hominid ancestor split from the great ape lineage when it split from its nearest cousin, chimpanzees.

So, the question begs to be asked: how come God created the universe 13,8 billion years ago and Earth 4,5 billion years ago, but then not only tries to hide these facts from us in his everlasting and truthful Word and Revelation (the Bible) but actively presents us with fake news about the design and timing?

When the irregularities and inconsistencies in the Bible started to jump at me, I needed an explanation to help me to keep up the faith. So, in my fervour to continue to believe in and commit to the biblical truths, I developed, not only for myself but to all who cared to listen, the following narrative: one of the reasons or necessities for the existence of the Holy Spirit was that he was there to reveal God to us, piecemeal over time. None of us was there when God created Earth, and none when Jesus was born of a virgin, walked on the Galilean waters and was raised from the dead. Someone needed to convince us of these things. I rationalised it as a necessary biblical growth-revelation on two levels. Firstly, for believers to grow nearer to God in their faith, they need the Holy Spirit's divine guidance along this growth path, to reveal God to them – incessantly but in small manageable doses. That is why true believers need to spend so much time delving into God's word and seeking His presence/face in prayer and meditation. Secondly, as science increasingly offers new information that needs to be reconciled with God's revelation, we need the Holy Spirit to guide us in our understanding and acceptance. For a while, this rational justification helped me to make peace with the inconsistencies and scientific and historical errors in the Bible.

In a sense, I have become addicted to history over the past fifteen years. This is ironic, as I remember vividly walking into

Mr Van Staden's history class in secondary school and being unable to hide my contempt for this boring subject of strange names and dates to be remembered. Going on to Standard Eight (Grade Ten), we had a choice of subjects at the time. I had to choose between a third language and history (or geology). I chose Latin (at the time, I still planned to study medicine and thought I needed Latin), which in hindsight, was a mistake for more than one reason. However, even though the language itself did nothing for me, it exposed me to Julius Caesar and the history of the Roman Empire, the Greek philosophers and the politics of their time. Maybe this was where my fascination with history started. Or maybe not – maybe it was in my genes because, as I have mentioned before, despite his total lack of formal education, my father had exceptional general knowledge, born from his hunger to read.

During my high school years, I read *The Iliad* by the ancient Greek poet Homer. Written in the mid-18th century, *The Iliad* is generally considered to be the earliest work in the whole Western literary tradition and one of the best-known and loved stories of all time. At the time, it more than captured my imagination. I was fascinated by the myth and the fantasy, the heroics of the men, the beauty and passion of Helena and the proactive involvement of the gods of the time in the everyday lives of the heroes of the day. The 2004 epic historical war film, *Troy*, is still one of my favourite movies.

So, in a sense, I see history and evolution as two sides of the same coin and view evolution as history playing itself out in slow-motion action.

7

Where I am today

(what's left of my final years)

I started this book by sharing my religious experiences with you. Everything in the first few chapters came quickly and naturally from memories of the earlier moments and events that determined the direction of the road I walked. I shared my journey's details – how I had grown into my religious conviction, passion and commitment, and how and why I grew out of that conviction. However, I have come to realise that my religious journey is far from over. My interest in the mechanisms and history of life on our "pale blue dot" continues to grow. There is so much to discover and learn, and I have more time on my hands now. In this final chapter, I want to share some compelling insights that fascinate me and keep me burning the midnight candle. Some topics covered in this chapter may initially seem remote from religion. Still, if you stay with me, I submit that you will see the connection and hope that you, too, will discover a fantastic world of wonder once you see and appreciate the most awesome bigger picture.

I have come to realise that in its various shapes and forms, religion has become an integral part of life on Earth and may never vacate its space. Maybe *Homo sapiens* may as well be called *Homo religiosis*, as the need for us to connect to something above and beyond ourselves seems inextricably part of the story-of-life we created and which became ingrained in our consciousness. However, I submit that religion must be seen and experienced in a context like everything else in life. Science has already disposed of most of the historical religious truths contained in the Bible and will incessantly continue to do so. However, it may not be able to close all the gaps in the very short time Sapiens has left in its search for reality.

Let's move on, and if you are not there yet, I hope you can open up your mind and tune down (just a bit) any preconceptions you may have, to be able to learn more of, and embrace, the wonder of the incredibly beautiful world and the life we have the unimaginably good fortune to be part of.

The scientific backdrop

In the previous chapter, I proposed that it was the mastering of language that propelled *Homo sapiens* to the top of the food chain and which "put *Homo sapiens* squarely in charge of further evolutionary trends – forever!" I need to elaborate on this because I have learned that the word "forever" is a word to be used with care, as it has many dimensions.

The dinosaurs occupied the pole position at the top of the food chain for several million years. Still, they never dominated the rest of the species as decisively as *Homo sapiens* managed to do in less than the 200,000 years of its existence. Actually, the subjugation of other species only took off around 12,000 years ago, with the domestication of some plants and animals. But today, it is impossible to imagine how any of the existing species can evolve to challenge Sapiens' total and utter control of most species' ongoing evolution.

The word "forever" often comes to mind when one considers the universe – the evolving universe. On the evening of 28 January 1948, BBC Radio broadcast a debate between one of the most potent intellectual forces of the twentieth century,

Bertrand Russell, and, equally well-known at the time, Jesuit priest Frederick Copleston.

The topic of the discussion: the existence of God.

Russell was a British polymath, philosopher, mathematician, historian, writer, social critic, political activist, and Nobel laureate. During the debate, he provided numerous arguments for questioning and rejecting the existence of a creator. One line of thought Russell pursued was this:[17]

> *So far as scientific evidence goes, the universe has crawled by slow stages to a somewhat pitiful result on this earth and is going to crawl by still more pitiful stages to a condition of universal death.*

With such a bleak outlook, Russell concluded:

> *... if this is to be taken as evidence of purpose, I can only say that the purpose is one that does not appeal to me. I see no reason, therefore, to believe in any sort of God.*

Bertrand Russell was not punting a philosophical argument here but instead held up a scientific fact. And this scientific fact is known as the Second Law of Thermodynamics. The law describes a fundamental characteristic inherent in all matter and energy, regardless of structure or form, whether animate or inanimate. In short, it declares that the production of waste, in any process whatsoever, is unavoidable and that everything in the universe, including us, has an overwhelming tendency to run down, to degrade, to wither. The future holds a continued deterioration, a relentless conversion of productive energy into useless heat, a steady draining, so to speak, of the batteries powering reality.

Nothing in the universe and nothing in any form of life is forever – a scientific fact!

The Second Law of Thermodynamics has been confirmed, over and over again and from different scientific perspectives. In some circles, it's even being referred to as "the law of life". All of the universe, every process and every object in it are subject to this relentless deterioration from order (low entropy) to disorder (high entropy) and inevitable long-term decay. Life in all form, shape and size will eventually disappear from this planet and everywhere else in the universe, wherever it may exist. An unrefutable scientific fact. The following is a side note, born from my religious background, as I ponder, tongue in cheek:

One must deduce that God's intention with and design of the afterlife was part of his eternal plan to preserve the crown of his creation "forever" – way beyond the existence of the universe. In addition, it is worth noting that this designed "forever-ness" of the crown of his creation is limited to *Homo sapiens*, excluding even their loving pets, e.g. their dogs, cats and birds. Finally, I have already alluded to the following, but remain hesitant to expound too much on it because it is a big jump for most to comprehend, but there are explicit scenarios on the table that give *Homo sapiens* precious little time left at the top of the food chain; and so, who will inherit the afterlife when another species/entity replaces *Homo sapiens*?

Let's move on to another fascinating observation. There is an interconnectedness of everything in the universe. We, they, them – everything and all – consist of atoms, the scientific formula of which today is mostly determinable and known (more about this later). Even though science today is still puzzled by consciousness and quantum mechanics, our knowledge is growing in leaps and bounds as we explore, discover and learn about these and other current frontiers defining life on Earth. God is steadily occupying a smaller and smaller part of the explanation on offer. The gaps in understanding the physics of the universe and how life started, evolved and is heading towards its final destination are being closed by science, and the "God-of-the-Gaps" is losing legitimacy. Allow me to explain:

The concept of the God-of-the-Gaps was first used by the influential Scottish scientist, explorer, church minister and evangelist Henry Drummond in his 1904 book *The Ascent of Man*. He believed that evolution was divinely guided, and employed arguments, provocative and controversial to both sides, to reconcile evolution with a creator God.

The God-of-the-Gaps strategy boils down to creationists (people who believe that God designed and created everything in the universe) proactively and eagerly seeking gaps in present-day knowledge and understanding of natural phenomena. If an apparent gap is found, it is assumed that God, by default, must fill it. Areas where there is still a lack of data or understanding are automatically considered to belong to God. Such episodes in the history of science are so common that the phrase God-of-the-Gaps was coined to label the process of invoking God to account for natural phenomena not yet explained by science. What worries thoughtful theologians (and there are increasingly more of them today) is that gaps shrink and disappear as scientific evidence advances. As scientists fill the gaps, God has less and less to do and is threatened with eventually having nothing more to do.

A famous example highlighting the God-of-the-Gaps concept involves two prominent scientists, Newton and De LaPlace, living a century apart.

Sir Isaac Newton (1643–1727) was an English mathematician, physicist, astronomer, theologian and author of the three-volume *Principia*, written in Latin and recognised by many as the greatest scientific work ever written. Although Newton probably closed more gaps than any other scientist, he also was a believer (as most people in his time were) and a devout Christian and occasionally invoked God in his explanations.

Newton clarified and refined the concept of universal gravity and devised mathematical equations to calculate the stupendous attractive force that celestial bodies have on objects in their immediate environment. His mathematical equations predict the motions of these bodies (e.g. the planets in our solar system) with extraordinary accuracy. All the planets in our solar system orbit the sun because of its size (mass) and, as a result, the massive gravitational attractive force it exerts on the planets. However, planets also exert a gravitational pull on one another, influencing their orbits around the sun. For example, when the earth passes Mars in its orbit around the sun, there is a small but significant gravitational interaction between Mars and Earth. Because Newton's formulas could calculate these tiny gravitational interactions, he was concerned about that. He thought that if these small interplanetary perturbations were to accumulate, they would eventually disrupt the smooth ongoing order of the solar system. Newton was a religious man and could not resist suggesting that God occasionally had to intervene to counter these disruptive forces and restore the magnificent order of the solar system. According to Newton, as discussed on the BioLogos[18] website, God's periodic interventions were needed to account for "the solar system's incredible ongoing stability".

In addition, the BioLogos site also shows that another universal phenomenon was unknown to Newton and the scientific world at the time – the process of how solar systems formed and evolved independently. In the decades after Newton, astronomers and physicists discovered that solar systems form naturally from enormous clouds of rotating matter. A large, slowly rotating cloud of stardust (hydrogen, helium, etc.) coalesces and collapses under its own gravity and tends to flatten into something like a giant pancake. Our own Saturn is an interesting example, where some of the cloud is still present and is observed as rings around the planet. Because the rotating matter in the gas cloud is not uniformly distributed, it collects (as a result of gravity) into big clumps in the plane of the pancake. After this process is completed, many millions of years later, we have a collection of clumps (celestial bodies) travelling in the same direction and the same plane – planets around their star, like our own solar system. Newton did not have the benefit of having observed and learned about this phenomenon, and so, according to him, "only God could have set things up so elegantly".

The BioLogos discussion concludes:

> *In both of these examples – one related to the ongoing motion of the planets and the other related to the origin of the motions – Newton is employing textbook God-of-the-gaps reasoning. Scientific theories are proposed to explain as much as possible, and then God is brought in to cover any remaining unexplained gaps in the explanation. We now know that Newton was wrong on both counts. The gravitational perturbations that planets experience are largely balanced to average out to near zero over time. The net result is that the planetary motions are extremely stable; they do not deteriorate over time. And it was a straightforward application of Newton's theory that (later on) revealed this. Newton simply had not done all the calculations to see if his intuition was right.*
>
> *The same was true for the orderly motion of the planets. Newton had no concept of how solar systems could form on their own or what the planetary motions would be like in naturally forming systems.*

The fallacy of this God-of-the-Gaps reasoning was prominently highlighted a hundred years later by a legendary conversation between the French physicist and mathematician Pierre-Simon de Laplace and the French emperor, Napoleon Bonaparte.

Laplace held a high-level bureaucratic post in Bonaparte's administration. He was the beneficiary of a century of progress by many scientists, refining and extending Newton's laws of motion and expanding the vision of what was going on in space. As a result, Laplace could draw on a hundred years of scientific and mathematical progress since Newton. He wrote a wide-ranging text (the five-volume *Celestial Mechanics*) explaining the workings of the heavenly bodies in much more detail than Newton. However, unlike Newton, Laplace never mentioned God in his writings or invoked divine intervention in describing the motions of the planets.

There are many anecdotes, created over the last two centuries, of the conversation that took place between Laplace and Bonaparte in 1802. Napoleon, who was fond of asking embarrassing questions and at the time was working hard to improve his relationship with the Pope, found it opportune to question Laplace about the absence of God in his theory. The setting may have been an elegant reception in Josephine Bonaparte's rose garden:

> *"Monsieur Laplace, they tell me you have written this large book on the functioning of the universe, and even though the greatest scientist of all time (Newton) has given credit to God on the subject, I am told that you did not even mention the Creator in your work."*

To this, Laplace famously replied:

> *"Monsieur Emperor, I had no need of that hypothesis."*

Even the great scientist, Isaac Newton, had used a deficiency in scientific explanation as an argument for God's existence. A hundred years later, science had cleared up that knowledge deficiency and had closed the gap, and the necessity for God to do something to keep his creation stable had disappeared.

For the newcomer to the interconnectedness of everything in the universe (including us), the following would be revealing, and I quote the American theoretical physicist, mathematician and string theorist, Brian Greene[19] where he says in his book, *Until the end of Time*:

Grind up anything previously alive, pry apart its complex molecular machinery, and you will find an abundance of the same six atoms: carbon, hydrogen, oxygen, nitrogen, phosphorus and sulfur, ...

Allow me to repeat this: the same six atoms are, without exception, abundantly present in every living organism on Earth, be it *Homo sapiens* or an oak tree. This, very obviously, begs two questions:

- What then, is the difference between a human being and an oak tree? Before dealing with this question, let's first consider the next question, which is far more exciting.
- Where do these atoms come from, and how did they end up on "our pale blue dot" *and* inside our bodies?

I cannot verbalise the incredible, wonderful world of awe that opened up for me over the past few years as I read about and came to understand the answers to these two questions.

To answer the second question, we need to backtrack a little. Let's start by considering the beauty of a clear southern African night sky if we look up and see the four stars of the Southern Cross and the countless other bright lights in our galaxy, the Milky Way. A galaxy is a group of stars or star systems (like our solar system), and there are millions of them in a galaxy or even billions in giant galaxies. The Milky Way gets its name from a Greek myth about the goddess Hera who sprayed milk across the sky. In other parts of the world, our galaxy goes by different names. In China, it's called the "Silver River", and in the Kalahari Desert in South Africa, it's aptly called the "The Backbone of Night".

The Milky Way is a mid-size galaxy in the known universe, and our solar system (our star, the Sun, and its eight orbiting planets and many moons) lies on the outer edge in one of its spiral arms. Our star is 26,000 light-years (2.5 x 10^{17} kilometres) from the centre of the Milky Way. A few years ago, astronomers discovered a supermassive black hole (named Sagittarius A*), 4 million times the mass of our Sun, at the heart of the Milky Way. As massive as this black hole is, its size still pales in comparison to the real monsters lurking in the centres of massive galaxies – up to 10 billion solar masses!

Interestingly, a spacecraft leaving Earth and our solar system will travel mostly in darkness through deep space because the light-giving stars are so far apart. However, if the spaceship approaches the centre of the Milky Way, it will most probably travel in indescribably brilliant light because of the abundance of stars at the centre – orbiting the black hole. The known universe consists of billions of galaxies, and because spacetime, according to Einstein, is curved, the universe has no centre. It expands in all directions from every vantage point. In his search to understand gravity, Albert Einstein connected three-dimensional space with time to create the four-dimensional concept of spacetime.

NASA launched its Voyager One spacecraft in 1977, travelling through deep space at 61,000 km/hr. Voyager One has already been "on the road" for 43 years and has covered more than 21 billion kilometres. If Voyager One were headed directly for the centre of our mid-size galaxy (which it is not), it would take the spaceship another 0,5 billion years to get there. How long will it take Voyager One to find the outer limits of an expanding universe consisting of billions of galaxies? Doesn't the word "forever" spring to mind here?

Consider the following: according to one estimate, the known universe consists of some hundred billion (10^{11}) galaxies, each with, on average, a billion stars. Still, it is so vast that it is mostly darkness and empty space, and – according to Carl Sagan – if you were to be randomly inserted into the universe from outside (wherever that may be), the chance or probability that you would find yourself on, or even near, any one of the multi-billions of planets, is one in a billion trillion trillion (10^{33}).

From a Biblical perspective, with tongue in cheek, one cannot help but reflect upon the vast space available to God to create an expansive and comfortable heaven and a king-size hell for the growing multitude of atheists.

A Belgian Catholic priest named Georges Lemaître first suggested the Big Bang theory in the 1920s, when he theorised that the universe began from a single primordial atom. A few years later, his idea received a major boost from the American astronomer Edwin Hubble. Hubble, working at the Mount Wilson Observatory in California, using a giant telescope at the time, observed that whole galaxies were speeding away from us – in all directions. Hubble's observations were repeatedly confirmed but received unequivocal confirmation with the 1965 discovery of cosmic microwave radiation by the physicists Arno Penzias and Robert Wilson. Scientists interpret these microwaves as echoes of the Big Bang still permeating the universe after 13,8 billion years.

However, the exact cause of the Big Bang is still an unsolved scientific question today. Newton's laws describe and capture – in mathematical equations – gravity as a force of attraction or pull. Einstein's theory of general relativity predicts that gravity can also be repulsive or push.

One of the hypotheses on the table is that the Big Bang was caused by repulsive gravity; in other words, the gravitational force that does not attract or pull but instead pushes. The Second Law of Thermodynamics tells us that entropy (disorder) is steadily increasing in the universe. The significant implication of this observation is that moving back in time to the beginning of time, the universe – or a part of the universe or even the tiniest part of the universe – must have been in a state of zero entropy (total order). Intuitively, this seems like a logical conclusion, but what was the condition of space before this moment?

Some cosmologists today consider the universe before the Big Bang a frantic and chaotic environment. They assume that the value of energy across space would have fluctuated wildly, somewhat like the surface of boiling water in a pot. To find a 100% flat piece (of water) on the body of the boiling water would have a stupendously low probability. And scientists are deeply uneasy without a good scientific explanation of how this extraordinary, uniform configuration could have been realised. Seeking relief from this discomfort, some researchers rely on a simple observation: if you wait long enough, even the most unlikely things will happen. God has not yet created time. To wait for a collection of atoms to align to perfect order, or zero entropy, was therefore not an issue, only a statistical probability – you wait long enough, and it will happen. Once again, the word "forever" comes to mind here. Especially so, as scientific theories contemplate that ours is not the first or the last universe; universes come and go. But let's not go there.

The mathematics to support this theory came many years later. While the gravitational force's capacity to be repulsive was known to Einstein, its most profound application was only discovered in 1979 by the American physicist and cosmologist Alan Guth. As explained by Brian Greene:

Guth realised, confirmed by his calculations, that if a region of space was filled with a particular kind of substance (cosmic fuel if you want) and if the energy contained within this substance was spread evenly throughout this region, then the resultant gravitational force would indeed be repulsive. Guth's calculations revealed that even if a tiny region, perhaps as small as a billionth of a billionth of a metre across, was saturated with uniformly distributed energy (zero entropy), the repulsive gravitational force would be enacted. Therefore, when a tiny speck of space finally made the statistically unlikely leap to zero entropy, repulsive energy jumped into action and propelled this tiny space into a rapidly expanding universe – the Big Bang.

The above is "heavy" science, so I have tried to keep it short. But let's move on to more understandable physics to get our heads around God's role in creating what we observe in our beautiful southern African night sky.

The Big Bang resulted in the formation of matter (mostly in gas form), energy, time and space 13,8 billion years ago. Immediately after the Big Bang, the universe could be described as an extremely hot plasma consisting of protons, electrons and photons. No atoms, as yet, existed. About 300,000 years later, as the expanding universe started to cool down, these enormous gas clouds coalesced and congealed. This led to the formation of the first atoms when the energy levels of protons and electrons became low enough to combine to form hydrogen. Hydrogen (consisting of one proton and one electron) is the first, lightest and most abundant element in the universe and even today, makes up 75% of the detectable content of the universe. None of the other elements of the periodic table existed at the time. God took his time with the rest of The Periodic Table of Elements, today's 118 elements. In fact, it took God forever (billions of years) to design and create the rest of the known elements. An element is a substance made entirely from one type of atom.

To consider the process of how God created some of the other elements, let's first consider what the early universe looked like. According to the Second Law of Thermodynamics, from a state of zero entropy (total order), repulsive gravity started our universe and created vast disorder (high entropy) in an infinitesimally short time. An indescribably large number of protons, neutrons and electrons were dispersed and moved through space at breakneck speeds. The distribution of these particles was not uniform, and increasingly so, as time passed and clouds of particles started to clump together under the gravitational force, which we know today as Newton's law.

These enormous clouds of mostly hydrogen atoms began to rotate and became denser as they moved through space. The larger the gas clouds were, the stronger the gravitational pull on surrounding particles and smaller gas clouds, and the bigger they became as they cleaned up their immediate environment. Consequently, the more massive they became, the stronger the gravitational force and crushing of the atoms in the core.

As the gravitational force started to crush the hydrogen atoms in the core of these massive celestial bodies, they became hotter and hotter. When the core temperature reached 10 million degrees, the hydrogen atoms fused and converted to helium. The resultant nuclear reaction sent a massive shock wave from the core to the surface, and billions of photons were spewed into space, creating a blinding light. Once the process started, it accelerated; millions of nuclear reactions followed, and the body became a fireball of atomic explosions. And so, about 200 million years after the Big Bang, the first star was born and lit up its very dark immediate environment.

If we consider this in Biblical terms, we read in Genesis 1:3-5 (New International Version), referring to Earth:

> *"And God said, "Let there be light," and there was light. God saw that the light was good, and he separated the light from the darkness. God called the light "day," and the darkness he called "night." And there was evening, and there was morning—the first day".*

Only with a small difference – our sun and earth were created around 9 billion years after the first light shined in the darkness of the universe.

Over time, the star's core turned to helium as it burned its hydrogen fuel. As the helium core grew bigger and bigger over time, the hydrogen moved outwards to cooler regions away from the hot helium centre of the star. Millions of stars followed as new ones were born every moment, across a vast universe, expanding at the speed of light. After millions of years, some stars burned out (used up all their nuclear hydrogen fuel) and died, and some bigger ones exploded as Supernovas. More about this later.

A few billion years after the first star was born in the universe, another mid-size star started to form. It was finally born around

4,5 billion years ago on the outskirts of one of the millions of galaxies already then dotting the cosmos. The galaxy eventually acquired the name "The Milky Way", and the star was baptised "Sun", sporting eight planets (excluding the dwarf planet Pluto) as companions in its sphere of gravitational influence.

Now we know how God created helium (the second element in the periodic table, with two protons, two neutrons and two electrons) through the fusion of hydrogen in the cores of stars. But what of the rest of the elements?

The bigger the star, the stronger the gravitational crushing force in the core and the hotter it runs. When the core of a big enough star, now consisting only of helium, reaches around a 100 million degrees, the helium atoms fuse to convert to the heavier carbon and oxygen elements. The helium now follows the hydrogen to the cooler outer regions of the fireball, with the heavier elements concentrated in the centre of the star. Incidentally, our star (Sun) is not big enough to follow this route and will most probably die in another 4 to 5 billion years without ever producing "fresh" carbon and oxygen in its core.

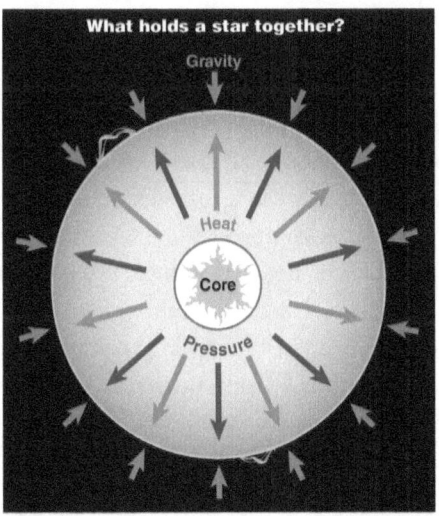

Figure 9 – What holds a star together? It's a balance of gravity pushing in on the star and heat and pressure pushing outward from the star's core.

The above process continues unabatedly; heavier and heavier elements are fused in the cores of massive stars. The shock waves created by the nuclear reactions in the core progressively push the lighter elements outwards towards the surface, and they are then spewed into space. When the core temperature reaches 3 billion degrees, the silicon nuclei now in the core fuse to become iron; once the core turns to iron (element 26 in the periodic table), fusion is mostly halted. Iron can fuse, but the process absorbs more energy than it releases and the core temperature drops.

Now we know how God created the elements up to number 26 in the periodic table, but what about the really heavy ones and precious metals like platinum and gold, etc.?

Once a star is formed, it is kept in balance between two opposite forces. The star's gravity tries to squeeze the star into the smallest, tightest ball possible. But the nuclear fuel burning in the star's core creates strong outward pressure. This outward push resists gravity's inward squeeze and maintains the star's equilibrium and stability.

When a massive star runs out of fuel, it cools down and effectively starts to die. This cooling down process causes the outward pressure to drop. Gravity wins out, and the star suddenly collapses. The collapse happens quickly, creating such enormous shock waves that the star's outer part explodes. This explosion is called a Supernova. A Supernova generates such stupendous energy that atoms of the heavier elements, e.g. gold, platinum and uranium, are created instantly and spewed into space. As described earlier, the process of forming massive celestial bodies (stars, planets, moons, etc.) from universal gas clouds repeats itself. The difference is that now these gas clouds contain a much wider variety of atomic elements, other than only hydrogen, like the first gas clouds.

Here's the thing: if Earth were one of the first planets formed after the Big Bang, there would not have been life-producing atoms like carbon, oxygen, nitrogen, etc., nor precious metal atoms like platinum and gold, present on "our pale blue dot". Earth is a newcomer in the evolving universe. Its formation depended upon the birth of millions of stars over more than 9 billion years and hundreds of thousands of subsequent star explosions (Supernovas) in its immediate environment. As a result, the massive universal gas clouds that formed our solar system, contained not only hydrogen (like the first-ever gas clouds after the Big Bang), but also the life-giving elements of carbon and oxygen, as well as precious metal elements like platinum, palladium and gold.

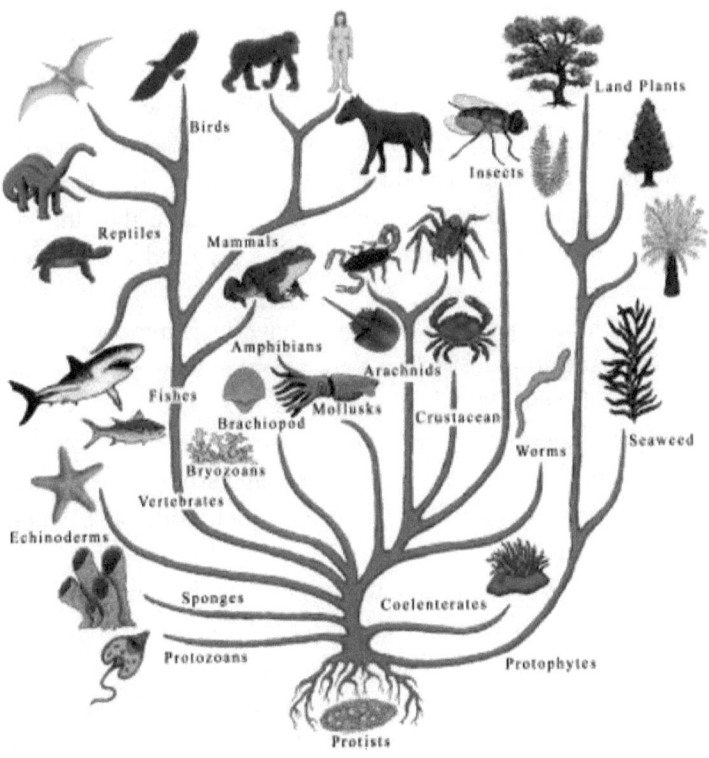

Figure 10 – Tree of life

Everything, but everything, on and inside this planet including us, *Homo sapiens* in body and brain (read mind), is totally and utterly, fully and completely, made up of stardust. Hundreds of thousands, if not millions of stars, had to die to create the atoms *Homo sapiens* are made of. Then about 3,8 billion years ago, our planet was ready for biology to be born and the replicator molecule to do its thing. God took his time (forever) to create the habitat of the crown of his creation.

This brings us to the first question we asked at the beginning of the chapter: what then is the difference between *Homo sapiens* and an oak tree?

From a biological perspective, the difference is a lot less than most people realise. We saw from the previous chapter that life first appeared around 700 million years after Earth was formed but mainly remained at the level of single-celled organisms (algae) for the next 3,3 billion years before the so-called Cambrian explosion brought about significant diversification. From my understanding, it seems fair to assume that the last common ancestor of humans and oak trees lived around 600 million years ago.

What humans and oak trees still have in common today is the fact that both consist primarily of water, as well as the fact that 70% of their DNA is identical.

They are interdependent – we breathe in oxygen and breathe out carbon dioxide, while trees take in carbon dioxide and release oxygen. If we weren't interdependent, one of us would not have been there.

The most significant difference between humans and oak trees is that oak trees (and other plants) can make their own food, while humans depend upon other living organisms to survive. There are, then, the obvious (and critical) differences of consciousness and language. Both have consciousness and language, just on different levels.

The major takeaway for me is the unbelievable

interconnectedness of all living organisms, all being descendants of this extraordinary replicating molecule that swam, probably all on its own, in the ocean 3,8 billion years ago.

The majestic story of an expanding and evolving universe and everything in and of it continues. If everything had a beginning, it must also have an end. Or does it? For example, do stars have infinite lives? Of course not. As we have seen earlier in this chapter, the Second Law of Thermodynamics predicts that all stars will eventually wither and die. Many of the stars we observe in our beautiful Southern African night sky are already dead. They may have died many years ago, but because light travels at a finite speed (300,000 km per second), it could take hundreds or even thousands of years for the last light emitted from the star to reach us. The death of the bigger stars produces black holes, today the most mesmerising objects in our universe but also the most mysterious.

A black hole is a region in space where the force of gravity is so strong that not even light, the fastest known entity in the universe, can escape. A black hole can not be directly observed because, from the outside, it has the same colour as deep space, i.e. pitch black, and nobody has ever seen (and most probably will never see) the inside of a black hole. A black hole is observed, and its position is defined by its event horizon and the accretion disc above the event horizon.

The event horizon of a black hole is the boundary or surface of the black hole or "point of no return", beyond which any matter crossing this line from outside will disappear and never return. The German astronomer and physicist Karl Schwarzschild was the first person convinced of the existence of black holes. In 1916 he developed a formula showing that the size of the event horizon was proportionate to the mass of the black hole. The Schwarzschild Radius defines the size of the event horizon (see Figure 11). Let us suppose an astronaut ever has the pleasure (or whatever you would call such an extraordinarily emotional experience) of approaching a black hole. In that case, he will look at, and as if into, a very, very black hole. If our astronaut becomes curious and ventures closer to have a peek inside and inadvertently crosses the "line" of the event horizon, something undescribable will happen to him. So remarkable that our mathematics and science today cannot describe what exactly will happen to him. What is certain, however, is that our astronaut will disappear, heading for the core at the "bottom" of the black hole (also called the singularity), and he will never, ever return, not in this life and not in the next. I don't think one could even say that he will be atomised; he will more probably be "quarkinised" (my inventive word) because, from my understanding, the particles that make up the core of the "body" at the centre of the black hole (the singularity) are orders of magnitude smaller than atoms, or even quarks (the smaller than small stuff that makes up protons, neutrons and electrons). The gravitational pull of the singularity on matter crossing the line of the event horizon is so immense that it cannot be described in known mathematical terms.

The accretion disk of a black hole is a rotational structure formed just above the event horizon in a region of space called the ergosphere, where matter starts to fall towards the event horizon and just before crossing the "point of no return" and disappearing into the black hole. The stupendous gravitational force of the black hole attracts all matter in its immediate environment towards it. The closer the objects (gas clouds, planets, stars, star systems, etc.) come to the event horizon, the faster they swirl in a whirlpool fashion as they resist the pull of the black hole and the hotter they become. The accretion disc can reach temperatures as hot as the hottest stars in the universe and emit powerful, luminous X-rays. These X-rays can be observed and used to identify and locate black holes. The black hole at the centre of our galaxy (the Milky Way) has an accretion disc 25 times larger than our solar system.

It is not yet possible to provide a clear definition of a black hole. A black hole seems to form at a place and a moment where two different and seemingly incompatible and conflicting theories of nature meet. One theory governs the very big (gravity, general relativity and celestial bodies), and the other the very small (the quantum mechanics of electrons, quarks and photons). Black holes are superlatively dense and, therefore, decidedly heavy but have quantum mechanical properties as the core of the black hole (the singularity) seems so small that it has no surface or volume. So, the densest and heaviest objects in the universe are also the most miniature objects in the universe. Physicists today believe that understanding black holes is our entry into combining these two seemingly independent theories. Scientists are looking for grand unifying equations or a "theory of everything", so to speak.

There are two main types of black holes, i.e. stellar black holes and supermassive black holes. A stellar black hole forms following a colossal cosmic explosion called a Supernova. A Supernova occurs when a massive star (ten to twenty times the mass of our Sun) dies and collapses. The star starts to die when it runs out of the nuclear fuel burning in its core. The equilibrium of the two forces sustaining the star is broken, and the outward pressure loses out against the inward gravitational force. The inward gravitational force now causes the inner part of the star

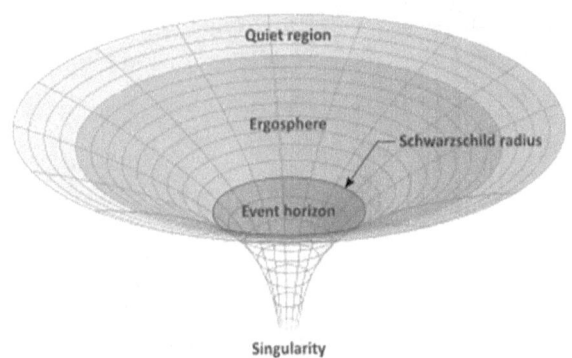

Figure 11 – An image of a black hole warping space.

to collapse instantly, and the outer part of the star explodes in a Supernova. After the stupendous nuclear explosion, blasting the star's outer regions into space, gravity crushes the inner part of the star into a singularity. The greatest part of the mass of the previously massive star has now become the smallest object imaginable, a thought we cannot as yet comprehend at all. The known scientific theories and mathematical equations break down at this point.

Supermassive black holes develop when galaxies and stellar black holes collide and merge, creating the most awesome objects in the universe. Supermassive black holes are so named because they contain singularities, millions to billions of times the mass of our sun. As far as we can tell, nearly every galaxy in the universe has one of these supermassive black holes sitting right at its centre, like a seed. And there is a correlation—a bigger galaxy has a bigger black hole, and a smaller galaxy has a smaller black hole. More and more black holes are being discovered, and cosmologists are already talking of billions of black holes in the universe.

Although first raised a century ago, black holes still elude scientific understanding, definition and quantification in mathematical equations. If you recall the "God of the Gaps" phantasm we discussed earlier in this chapter, you will recognise that this concept is a sure candidate for God to receive credit for the mystery of black holes – at least for the time being until science provides an explanation.

The religious backdrop

Even before I had my second Saul of Tarsus Damascene Road moment (you will remember that it wasn't exactly a blinding-light experience, but rather a slow and hesitant journey), I started reading Christian religion outside the Bible. I read some of the apocryphal books, including the Gospels of Mary Magdalene and Judas (Iscariot) and Thomas, and some of the Maccabees' stories. Not much inspiring or revealing resulted from most of these, other than me pondering what a fight it must have been among the clerics at Nicaea in 325 to decide which books to include and which to exclude from the final Bible. There seem to have been many opinions and interpretations over a thousand years, which is still evident today as the Roman Catholic Bible contains seventy-three books, and the Protestant Bible has sixty-six books.

The Christian religion was growing in leaps and bounds during the 3rd and 4th centuries, but there were many sects with wide-ranging differences and doctrines, not least of which was the actual status of Jesus as the son of God. For Constantine, the Roman emperor (280 – 337), "unity was the mother of order", and he was dismayed by the escalating strive and in-fighting among a growing portion of his subjects. He ordered some senior bishops to call a meeting, sort out the internal disagreements, and conclude and confirm what exactly constitutes the Christian religion. An invitation went out to 1800 bishops from all over the Roman world to meet at Nicaea (today Iznik in Turkey). Only around 300 eventually arrived with over 1200 assistants, i.e. priests and deacons. Long journeys were difficult and dangerous in those days. After seven weeks of discussion and debate, the first ecumenical council of the Christian church in 325 came up with the Nicene Creed, which among other things, defines the nature of the relationship between God the Father and God the Son. The Nicene Creed mentioned the Holy Spirit, but it was only at the ecumenical council of Constantinople in 381 that the Holy Spirit was confirmed as an inherent part of the Trinity God. A classic yet modern example of how the man-made image of God changes over time. However, the exact nature of the Holy Spirit as an intrinsic part of the Trinity God remains a contentious issue to this day. It was a contributing factor which led to the Great Schism in 1054 between the Western and Eastern Christian churches.

I want to share some insights from the *Gospel of Judas*. The Gospel of Judas is one of many so-called apocryphal books, which means that it did not make it to the final Bible because the clerics judged it in the 4th century not to have been inspired by God. Sometime in the 1970s, a copy of the *Gospel of Judas*, translated into Coptic from its original second-century Greek, was found in Middle Egypt near Al Minya. After moving from dealer to dealer, place to place and improperly stored in between, the original text, at last, ended up in safe hands and was restored as close as possible to its original condition. And in April 2006, this extraordinary archaeological find was finally made public by the National Geographic Society.

The *Gospel of Judas* was written around 150 CE and, as with the canonical Gospels, was written many years after the events and therefore not by the men to whom they were attributed. It is, however, clear that the historians knew about this document, as the church father Irenaeus, in 180 CE, wrote stingingly against the *Gospel of Judas*.

I want to highlight two issues from *The Gospel of Judas*, which stood out. Because I do not have the skills and experience to read and meaningfully interpret a direct translation of such an old text (Karen L King translated the *Gospel of Judas* from the Coptic into English), I prefer to rely on the insights and comments of scholars and experts in these cases.

According to Christopher Hitchens in his book, *God is Not Great*:

> *The book is chiefly spiritualist drivel, as one might expect, but it offers a version of "events" that is fractionally more credible than the official account.*

Hitchens gives two reasons:

- The author of the Gospel maintains that the god of the Old Testament is a false god and should not be followed. He should be avoided because of his sickly insistence on bloody and violent sacrifice, both animal and human, even child sacrifice.

Elaine Pagels and Karen King (*Reading Judas – The Gospel of Judas and the Shaping of Christianity*)[20] concur and comment on the relevant text (Judas 5:1–19):

> *All the immoral acts and violence they witnessed in the dream result from worshipping the lower "God", who uses Jesus's name to set himself up falsely as the true God. It is this lower "God" who demands sacrifices, but he is merely a "minister of error" (5:15). Jesus calls upon his disciples to stop this behavior, to quit sacrificing themselves and others to this false "God" …*

- The author further claims that Jesus promoted Judas over the other disciples because Judas alone recognised who Jesus really was, and understood what was at stake and what needed to follow. The other disciples were bewildered and had no idea what was going on.

Elaine Pagels and Karen King concur when Judas tells Jesus (Judas 2:22–24):

> *"I know who you are and which place you came from – you came from the realm of the immortal Barbelo – but I am not worthy to proclaim the name of the one who sent you."*

Now, this "Barbelo" was not a father god but a heavenly destination, a kind of motherland beyond the stars. According to Judas, Jesus came from this celestial realm and was not the son of Jahwe, the god created by Moses with his overzealous and extremist human characteristics (El was the god worshipped by the Israelites before Moses discovered Jahwe at the burning bush). Recognising that Judas had more insight than the others, Jesus then took Judas aside and awarded him the unique mission of helping him to shed his fleshly form and return heavenward. Jesus also promised to show Judas the stars that would enable him to follow on.

Christopher Hitchens concludes:

> *Deranged science fiction though this is, it makes infinitely more sense than the everlasting curse placed on Judas for doing what somebody had to do ... It also makes infinitely more sense than blaming the Jews for all eternity.*

In my later years, I familiarised myself with other religions by reading about the Buddha, Confucius, Zoroaster, the Hindu Vedics and Upanishads and Islam. The more I read about other deities and the cultural and socio-economic environments which sustain them, the more I realised how God evolved as a human creation and not the other way around. People surviving in different environments create different gods to meet different needs. And over time, even the attributes of the created gods change or are replaced by other gods as settings and conditions change. In the past, groups of people were more isolated, and each grouping had its god or gods attending to its specific needs. There was a multitude of gods then. In our more globalised and high-tech world today, the planet is a smaller place with a smaller variety of needs and a better understanding of our needs (who and what we are, where we came from and where we are going). As a result, far fewer gods.

The above was my wisdom until I read Karen Armstrong,[21] one of the world's most prominent religious scholars. She says:

> *When I began to research this history of the idea and experience of God in the three related monotheistic faiths of Judaism, Christianity and Islam, I expected to find that God had simply been a projection of human needs and desires. I thought that 'he' would mirror the fears and yearnings of society at each stage of its development. My predictions*

were not entirely unjustified but I have been extremely surprised by some of my findings ... It would have saved me a great deal of anxiety to hear – from eminent monotheists in all three faiths – that instead of waiting for God to descend from on high, I should deliberately create a sense of him for myself. Other Rabbis, priests and Sufis would have taken me to task for assuming that God was – in any sense – a reality 'out there'; they would have warned me not to expect to experience him as an objective fact that could be discovered by the ordinary rational process. They would have told me that in an important sense God was a product of the creative imagination, like ... poetry and music ... A few highly respected monotheists would have told me quietly and firmly that God did not really exist – and yet that 'he' was the most important reality in the world.

What to make of this?

Let's go back in time and find the first image of God – if that is possible. I suspect that there are many "first" images of God, but I will share with you the one I find compelling. It is a rock painting in one of the Volp caves situated in the foothills of the Pyrenees mountains between France and Spain. Three French brothers accidentally discovered the limestone caves, created by the Volp River's persistence, in 1912. The cave complex consists of three interconnecting chambers which bore their names, Enlene, Les Trois-Freres and Tuc d'Audoubert.

The caves were first studied by the French archaeologist and priest Henri Breuil, who meticulously noted and copied most of the multitude of images he found inside. Reza Aslan, interprets Breuil's findings as part of a spiritual journey, tens of thousands of years ago, of our historical ancestors: *Homo sapiens* or "the wise human" – Adam and Eve, if you will.

In his book, *God: A Human History of Religion*, Aslan discusses Adam and Eve's short religious journey, which would have started in a pre-chamber named Salle des Morts. Archaeological finds suggest that the worshippers had gathered to consecrate themselves before entering the main cave complex. Evidence of sunken hearths of burning animal bone, widely believed to possess a mediating power, is found here. In some societies, shamans or priests would use the remains of burned animal bones for scrying. Aslan says:

> *Burning animal bone in these hearths is [also] likely a means of absorbing the essence of the animal.*

Adam and Eve were much closer to, had a lot more respect for, and felt themselves much more at one with animals and nature than their descendants today. Aslan continues:

> *The overpowering aroma of smoldering bone and marrow in such a confined space acts as a kind of incense meant to consecrate those gathered here. Picture Adam and Eve sitting in this antechamber for hours at a time, swathed in smoke, swaying with their kin to the pounding rhythm of animal-hide drums, the tinny echo of flutes carved from vulture bones, and the ting of xylophones constructed from polished flint blades – all of which have been discovered in and around caves like these – until they achieve the sanctified state necessary to continue on their journey.*

Albeit in different forms, this consecrating ritual rings true, as – even today – it is still widely practised when worshippers gather. Since antiquity, worshippers across the religious spectrum have employed incense in their sacred ceremonies. The Roman Catholic and Eastern Orthodox Christian churches were well known for burning frankincense, but many other Christian denominations followed in later years. Burning incense is viewed as a different form of prayer. The scent of frankincense permeates the whole church from the front to the back and, like prayers, rises to heaven. The spiritual idea is that, like incense, what is holy permeates the world around us.

For twenty-five years, before every church service, twice on any given Sunday, I had gathered with all the church council members in a pre-chamber, the consistory. After dealing with organisational matters, we consecrated ourselves with two prayers, one from a Deacon and one from an Elder, before marching solemnly into the main assembly. The preacher would be the last to enter but would stop for silent prayer before ascending the pulpit.

After consecration, Adam and Eve would have proceeded through the first chamber to the second, Les Trois-Freres, and found themselves in the main assembly of their "church". Here they would have encountered rock art, which, according to anthropologists, so clearly defines their spiritual life. The rock art in this part of Les Trois-Freres consists mainly of dots and handprints. Row upon row of black and red dots of various sizes in one section and dozens of handprints in another section of the chamber. No one knows the real meaning of the dots, but according to Aslan:

Figure 12 – Interpretation of positive and negative handprints found in Cuava de las Manos, Santa Cruz, Argentina (ca 15,000 to 11,000 BCE)

> *[T]he dots ... are often painted in a clearly perceptible pattern that is repeated from chamber to chamber. That suggests the dots may be a form of communication or instruction, a kind of code relaying some vital information to the [worshippers] as they continue journeying deeper into the bowels of the earth.*

Handprints are by far the most ubiquitous and instantly recognisable form of rock art in the world today. The oldest handprints go back some 39,000 years and are found virtually all over the world. The prints are positive and negative, i.e. made either by dipping the hand into wet pigment and pressing it against the cave wall or placing the hand against the wall and using a hollowed-out bone to spray the paint around it to create a shadow.

Adam and Eve would then have continued their journey into the very heart of the cave and entered a small, cramped room tucked away in a nearly inaccessible corner of the complex. Here the walls are covered with hundreds of brightly coloured images of animals, some drawn and some incised into the rock. Many are superimposed, one on top of the other in a frozen frenzy of activity: bison and bears and horses, reindeer and mammoths, stags and ibexes. Some are mysterious and unidentifiable, and many are a mixture of human and animal. According to Aslan:

> *It is not exactly correct to call these drawings "images." They are, like the dots and the handprints, symbols reflecting our ancient ancestors' animistic belief that all living things are interconnected, that they all share in the same universal spirit...*
>
> *The drawings are often tucked between pillars or otherwise placed in a position that allows them to be viewed only from certain angles and only by a handful of people at a time, indicating that the cave – not just the images projected upon it, but the cave itself – was intended to be part of the spiritual experience. The cave becomes a* mythogram; *it is meant to be* read, *the way one reads scripture.*

If the pathway through the Volp caves was a form of scripture, then Adam and Eve were about to reach the keynote of their pilgrimage. They would have crawled through another narrow tunnel, which curved upwards and led onto a narrow ledge a couple of metres above the cave floor. A few metres further, the ledge widens, and here they would have straightened up and turned to look up, face the ceiling, and witness the crowning image of the complex.

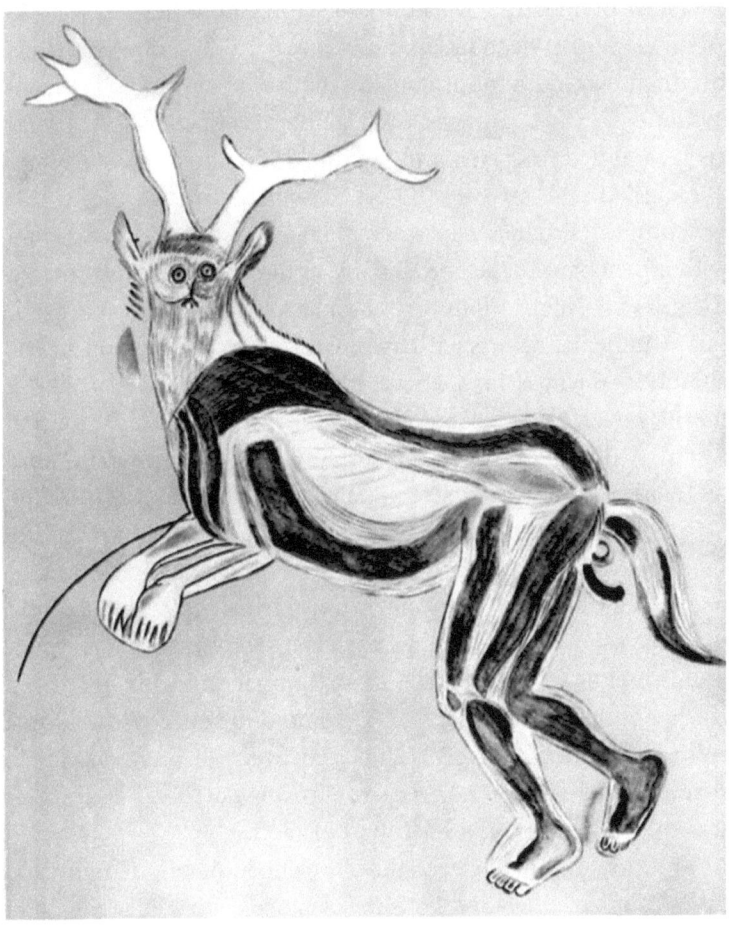

Figure 13 – The Sorcerer (Interpretation of a drawing by Henri Breuil) Les Trois-Freres, Montesquieu-Avantes, France (ca. 18,000 to 16,000 BCE)

And Adam and Eve may have been looking at the first-ever image of God, created by *Homo sapiens* around 20,000 years ago.

The image is that of a man – that much is certain. But it is something more. It has the legs and feet of a human but the ears of a stag and the eyes of an owl. It has a long bushy beard and two wrought antlers jutting from its head. Its hands look like the claws of a bear, and its muscular torso and thighs belong to an antelope. Between its hind legs is a sizeable semi-erect penis curving upwards, almost touching the horsetail protruding from its buttocks. The figure is both painted and engraved. It has been modified, redrawn and repainted, for thousands of years.

Henri Breuil saw this figure as a cult image meant for veneration, perhaps even worship. Breuil was a religious man with a penchant for seeing divinity in unexplained phenomena. Even so, a single, dominant humanoid figure set apart like this is unheard of in such caves. Moreover, its location in the chamber, elevated high above eye level, makes it seem like it presides over the other animals in the cave. At first, Breuil had assumed that the figure was a shaman dressed in some kind of hybrid animal costume, which is why he named it "The Sorcerer", and the name had stuck. In ancient communities, shamans were thought to have had one foot in this world and one foot in the next. They could move from the material world to the spirit world and bring back messages from the beyond, usually with the assistance of an animal guide. After some consideration, Breuil changed his mind and concluded that this strange creature staring back at him from on high was not a shaman or a sorcerer. As he wrote in his notebook in 1931, it was the earliest image ever found of God.

The god Breuil believed he had encountered in the Volp caves is one of the oldest gods in religious history. It is generally known as what religious scholars refer to as the Lord of Beasts or the Master of Animals. It probably was the first deity ever conceived of, as it was worshipped as the ruler or guardian of the forests. Hunters prayed to this god and soothed him with offerings to help with the hunt. It had the power to release animals into the wild for hunting, or make them disappear if it was angry with the hunters. This god was part of nature and one with the animals. The animals' souls belonged to this god, and when they were hunted and killed, it collected the souls back to itself. Versions of this god existed in nearly every part of the world.

The scientific debate over the origins of religion started in earnest in the nineteenth century as a natural progression of the European post-Enlightenment movement. Questions about everything, including the divine, were subjected to reasoned analysis and scientific scrutiny. It was also the era of Charles Darwin and evolutionary theory, which caused a major upset in the conventional wisdom of the day. Archaeological discoveries over the past 150 years and anthropological studies contributed significant insight. It has been a long and winding road, but we have come a long way in understanding the origin and makeup of the religious impulse.

- The English anthropologist Edward Burnett Taylor (1832–1917) suggested that the source of the religious impulse and the behaviours that arise from it are to be found in the belief that a "soul" exists separate from the body. Taylor's take was that "dreams" enacted this awareness of a soul. He theorised that if Adam runs into his dead father in a dream, he would be tempted to think that his father is still alive, albeit in a different form or shape. Not all of Taylor's contemporaries agreed with his dream hypothesis.

- Max Müller (1823–1900), Taylor's German counterpart, tried to show how different societies and nations arrive, along different paths, at a belief in a soul. He believed that humanity's first religious awareness resulted from encounters with nature. Primitive people looked at the sky and wanted to understand its workings. Day and night follow one another without fail, as do the seasons. So does the moon, as it changes form in its approximately 30-day cycle in perfect rhythm. At times there was perfect harmony; at other times total chaos – volcanic eruptions, tsunamis, sweltering heat, droughts, fires and obliterating storms. Someone or something must be responsible. Sometimes benevolent and sometimes angry.

I want to add the following to this line of thought: Primitive people looked at life and could not understand why some lives were short, and some were long, some people were lucky and survived predators, and some were unlucky and were eaten early in life, some were born sick/weak/deformed, others healthy/strong/perfect. Some groups or families were annihilated by other groups, and some groups or families prevailed. Someone or something must have an influence on these things? And the crowning question of all – what happens to you when you die?

- The British ethnologist and anthropologist Robert Marrett (1866–1943) punted animism, arguing that Adam and Eve believed in an invisible force, a kind of universal soul, which he called "mana", which represents the supernatural force that exists in all objects.

- The French sociologist, Émile Durkheim (1858–1917), submitted that religion was "an eminently social thing" and proposed that the religious impulse must have been grounded in social life, i.e. in the rites and rituals that helped a community develop a collective consciousness. A consciousness that was nurtured by creating fiction and propagating storytelling.

Whatever it was that enacted the religious impulse, I think it is fair to say that the belief of a soul as a separate entity from the body has, in one form or another, been present in every society, in every culture, and throughout time, and is probably the most common denominator in most faiths.

The existence of a higher presence, a power, a force or whatever, made a lot of sense to primitive people who did not benefit from the knowledge brought forth by science – which reared its head only 500 years ago. There is no doubt that for a great many people over many thousands of years, some form of religion helped make sense of a mystifying and volatile existence. And it seems fair to say that that may very well still be true today. Christopher Hitchens has an opinion on this when he says:

> *"Sigmund Freud was quite correct to describe the religious impulse, in* The Future of an Illusion, *as essentially ineradicable until or unless the human species can conquer its fear of death and its tendency to wish-thinking."*

Conclusion

> *Daar is geen sin in die lewe nie.*
> *– Die sin wat daar is,*
> *is die sin wat jy aan jou lewe gee.*

I wrote the above piece inside the cover of a book (*Homo Deus* by Yuval Noah Harari) I gave to my eldest daughter and son-in-law about two years ago. It is the logical conclusion anyone will arrive at who understands evolution by natural selection. However, I have subsequently reflected a lot on this statement, and as real as it is, I have come to realise that there is a non-rational and emotional dimension to it that requires empathy.

To be even-handed, one must accept that for some people, the meaning and purpose of their lives is their religion. Even though for most churchgoers, their religiosity has far more in common with a social club than a way of life focused on and dedicated to their Lord in the first place and equally to others. I have crossed paths with a handful of believers for whom their faith truly is the meaning and purpose of their lives. And I have learned to respect that. I hope I have become more considerate about not offending those people when expressing my opinion on religious matters. However, it is challenging at times, when observing the general apathy, ignorance and naivety, but also sometimes the raw selfishness cloaked in hypocrisy.

Following my liberation from religious doctrines, there was a short time during which I was very keen to share my enlightenment and newfound wisdom with everybody. I very quickly found out that this was an absolute no-no. I caught on that nobody wants to hear or learn that he or she is indoctrinated, superstitious, naïve, or – worst of all – ignorant. Even if proven accurate, proud people will defend their lives against such accusations.

I often wonder how many pastors, ministers, priests, etc., had not, at some stage in their careers, arrived at the same conclusion as I had. Consider this: "predikante" (ministers in the three Afrikaans churches) graduate from the university after seven years of full-time study – these are not your average graduates! I know of quite a few Afrikaans churches' ministers who have lost their faith, openly admitted it, and walked away from the rational god of the Bible and the eternal truths proclaimed in it. But I would not be surprised if a significant number have had a similar journey but are not prepared to, or – even worse – cannot afford to admit and make it known, not least of all for financial reasons. It may also be that many of them had, at some stage, concluded that this fictional story created by *Homo sapiens* is based on wishful thinking but sincerely still believe that it would do more harm than good to reveal the truth. And instead, prefer to continue to be a perceived anchor and bearer of hope, even if this hope is based on a fantasy. Sir James Frazer, in his famous study of religion and magic, *The*

Golden Bough, suggests that the novice witch doctor is better off if he does not share the illusions of his ignorant congregation. For one thing, if he does take the magic literally, he is much more likely to make a career-ending mistake. Better to be a cynic and tell yourself that everybody is better off in the end.

There is another way of looking at this. I alluded to it when describing my second faith-healing experience in Chapter 5:

> *Because part of me wanted it to work, I knew that for any remote chance of success whatsoever, from a psychological point of view, I at least had to cooperate. So, at some advanced stage of the proceedings, I closed my eyes and focused on his appeals to Jesus.*

From my understanding, this phenomenon goes by various names and is defined and verbalised differently, but it all boils down to manipulating the mind. The American church minister Norman Vincent Peale referred to it as "The Power of Positive Thinking" in his 1952 book of the same name. Even though some mental health experts criticised his philosophy, his book became a bestseller and developed a wide following.

In the same vein, Professor Daniel Dennett, an American philosopher, writer, and cognitive scientist, attracted much attention for his "natural science" explanation of religion. He promulgates his "belief in belief" philosophy and shows that it is a common phenomenon not restricted to religion.[22] For example, economists realise that a sound currency depends on people believing that the currency is sound. Dennett ponders if even 10% of the people who proclaim their belief in God actually do believe in God. For example, the actions of most, if not all, preachers and politicians are focused on fostering and protecting those beliefs and, in doing so, serving their own interests. According to Dennett, that's acting on "belief in belief".

Considering the "placebo effect", it seems the medical world does not reject this line of thought either. Therefore, in the psychological arena, it seems possible that some people can be better off believing in something than in nothing, however untrue that something may be. In other words, those who believe in the faith healer, witch doctor or shaman's cure have better morale and, therefore a higher chance of actually being cured.

Christopher Hitchens concurs and sums it up when he says:

> *Some of this will always be disputed among anthropologists and other scientists, but what interests me and always has is this: Do the preachers and prophets also believe, or do they too just "believe in belief"? Do they ever think to themselves, this is too easy? And do they then rationalize the trick by saying that either (a) if these wretches weren't listening to me they'd be in even worse shape; or (b) that if it doesn't do them any good then it still can't be doing them much harm?*

I paraphrase Yuval Harari when he ponders, tongue in cheek: There are two kinds of gods in this world, and people tend to mix them up. One, there is the "mystery god" about which we know and understand nothing. This mysterious god is the owner of the answers to a handful of questions that science is not yet capable of answering, for instance, what process started the Big Bang, how life began on Earth, or what constitutes the singularity at the centre of a black hole. This mystery god is majestic in his presence as we observe him in the universe, but he is far away, out there, and not at all involved in the details and day-to-day management of his creation. Harari is perfectly happy to believe in this god.

Then there is his opposite, the concrete "lawgiver god", about whom we know far too much. We know, for example, precisely what he thinks about female fashion and human sexuality. He knows when and who our children should marry, especially our daughters. We know this god has a dim view of abortions and hates same-sex marriages, irrespective of the resulting trauma, suffering, sorrow and heartache people will experience if these options are negated by the man-made laws of this all-loving god. Ironically though, he is nice enough to bless whatever excesses we allow ourselves at the dinner table, as long as we thank him for it. We know that he is hypersensitive to criticism but loves eminence and honour. So we grovel at his feet, proclaiming our unworthiness, heaping as much praise upon him as we can muster to soothe his ego. And, to top it all, if we follow his instructions and praise him enough, he may be willing to help us win the rugby world cup against the All Blacks.

Harari abhors this god (and so do I), for the simple reason that this god is the collective product of our fantasies, weaknesses, insecurities and prejudices.

I gave my children that book towards the end of a traumatic religious experience they had. They were caught up in a religious cult in Pretoria East for six years before wrestling themselves free. I use the word wrestle because I can clearly remember the exhausting hours and nights of discussion we had during this time. I was not instrumental in their decision to part with this church, but I helped give them a perspective on what had happened and how to move on. My daughter has started to pen their experiences, and I hope she can find the time to finish her book and get closure on a bad experience and a wasted six years of their lives.

Let's finally consider the issue of religion and morality. As a baby boomer growing up in South Africa, I was exposed continuously to scary stories of communists as devilish unbelievers and atheists. Communism was the twin brother of satanism, and the strong man in the Kremlin was akin to the antichrist. The USSR was that extraordinarily evil empire whose only aim was to rule the world and force the good people of the west and the believing world to surrender their faith. We were imbued with the firm belief that once the communists took over, they would ban the Bible and close down the churches; anarchy would ensue, and total lawlessness would be the order of the day. None of us knew anything about communism, but we were dead scared of this potent evil threatening our society's good order. Our government at the time harvested richly from this narrative and kept feeding us with the belief that communism equals atheism, which equals a total breakdown in moral standards and ethics. Fortunately, this storyline was mortally wounded when the Wall came down in 1989, and the fear of societal moral collapse as a consequence of communism has now disappeared. Although, as far as I am aware, real communism (Marxism) has never been practised anywhere in the world. The Bolsheviks hijacked communism, and Stalin and his followers ran dictatorships. The ruling elite in China call themselves The Communist Party, but Karl Marx would turn in his grave, should he hear this. China has more billionaires than the USA today. It minted more than 250 new billionaires over the past year alone. Either way, the point here is that morality and ethical behaviour are not linked, in any way, to political or religious orientations.

However, it appears that many, if not most, religious people really believe religion is what motivates them to be good. They find it hard to imagine how, without faith, one can be good or even want to be good. Michael Shermer, in his book *The Science of Good and Evil*, sums it up neatly as he says (as paraphrased by Richard Dawkins in *The God Delusion*):

> *If you agree that, in the absence of God, you would [likely] "commit robbery, rape and murder", you reveal yourself as an immoral person... If, on the other hand, you admit that you would [likely] continue to be a good person even when not under divine surveillance, you have fatally undermined your claim that God is necessary for [you] to be good.*

There is absolutely no evidence at all to suggest that believers (pick your religion) behave more or less ethically and morally than non-believers.

Most of Western Europe had already walked away from the rational god of the Bible a century ago, without – in my opinion – losing any of its sense of morality and ethics. Having lived in Germany for the past sixteen years, I would say quite the opposite. Humanism – the ethical system that goes with atheism – which is the prevailing social order in most parts of middle Europe, fosters a more mutually respectful and less opportunistic winner-takes-all environment. Human rights are entrenched and inalienable, which seems to me, after generations, to make for less aggression and higher tolerance in society. It may partly explain why South Africa, today, is an abnormally aggressive and violent society. Until only a couple of decades ago, we held the Bible up as our guiding light but frowned starkly upon human rights.

It took a while, but today I feel comfortable calling myself an atheist. I think of myself as free-thinking, not bound by religious indoctrination, superstition or wishful thinking.

Then again, I have learned that even atheism is a relative concept. GOD has manifested itself as one of the greatest and most enduring stories ever created by *Homo sapiens*. As with all created stories, the concept of god has changed over millennia to keep it real and workable for the people at the time. And atheism has been there all along, hitching a ride; as the concept of god changes, it forces the concept of atheism to change. Even only referring to the three monotheistic religions, Jews, Christians and Muslims were all at one stage called "atheists" by their pagan contemporaries. Modern atheism may only be a temporary denial of a god that is no longer adequate to the problems of our time and will change if and when a more relevant notion of god emerges. I have no problem with this; I am open to change, as there is so much to learn and discover.

References and notes

[1] Yuval Noah Harari, *Sapiens: A Brief History of Humankind* (London: Vintage Books, 2014).

[2] Christopher Hitchens, *God is Not Great* (London: Atlantic Books, 2008).

[3] "Patterns of African and Asian admixture in the Afrikaner population of South Africa." An article published on Feb. 24, 2020, by BMC Biology, part of Springer Nature.

[4] Gleb Bryanski, "Russian patriarch calls Putin era 'miracle of God'". An article published on Feb. 8, 2012, by Reuters World News.

[5] Leonid Laparenok, "Prominent Russians: Vladimir I". An article from RT.Com Russiapedia.

[6] Javier Corrales (Professor of political science at Amherst College), "A Perfect Marriage: Evangelicals and Conservatives in Latin America". An article published on Jan. 17, 2018, in the *New York Times*.

[7] Reza Aslan, *God: A Human History of Religion* (London: Penguin Corgi Edition, 2018).

[8] Richard Dawkins, *The God Delusion* (London: Penguin Black Swan Edition, 2016).

[9] Robin MacKie, *Ape-Man: The Story of Human Evolution* (London: BBC Worldwide Ltd, 2000)

[10] https://en.wikipedia.org/wiki/Galileo_affair

[11a] Edgar B. Herwick III, WGBH Radio Station, Boston Massachusetts, March 20, 2014

In the early 1950s, Pope Pius XII not only declared that the big bang and the Catholic concept of creation were compatible; he embraced Lemaître's idea as scientific validation for the existence of God and of Catholicism.

[11b] Doug Linder, *The Vatican's View of Evolution: The Story of Two Popes*, 2004.

In 1951, interestingly, Pius XII (who so grudgingly acknowledged the possibility of evolution) celebrated news from the world of science that the universe might have been created in a Big Bang. (The term, first employed by astronomer Fred Hoyle was meant to be derisive, but it stuck.) In a speech before the Pontifical Academy of Sciences he offered an enthusiastic endorsement of the theory: "…it would seem that present-day science, with one sweep back across the centuries, has succeeded in bearing witness to the august instant of the primordial Fiat Lux [Let there be Light], when along with matter, there burst forth from nothing a sea of light and radiation, and the elements split and churned and formed into millions of galaxies." (ME, 254-55) (ME – Measuring Eternity, Martin Gorst, 2001)

But the Pope didn't stop there. He went on to express the surprising conclusion that the Big Bang proved the existence of God:

Thus, with that concreteness which is characteristic of physical proofs, [science] has confirmed the contingency of the universe and also the well-founded deduction as to the epoch when the world came forth from the hands of the Creator. Hence, creation took place. We say: therefore, there is a Creator. Therefore, God exists!

[12] Ann Druyan, *Cosmos - Possible Worlds* (New York: National Geographic, 2020).

[13] Carl Sagan, *Cosmos* (New York: Ballantine Books, 2013).

[14] Richard Dawkins, *The Selfish Gene* (Oxford: University Press, 40th Anniversary Edition, 2016).

[15] Peter Farley – article from Yale Medicine Magazine https://medicine.yale.edu/news/yale-medicine-magazine/a-theory-abandoned-but-still-compelling/

[16] Daniel Toker, "A Bundle of Thoughts" – article from the *Brain Scientist* https://thebrainscientist.com/2018/04/11/you-dont-have-a-lizard-brain/

[17] Bertrand Russell, *Why I Am Not a Christian* (New York: Simon & Schuster, 1957).

[18] https://biologos.org/common-questions/are-gaps-in-scientific-knowledge-evidence-for-god/

[19] Brian Greene, *Until the End of Time* (New York: Alfred A Knopf Books, 2020).

[20] Elaine Pagels & Karen L King, Reading Judas – *The Gospel of Judas and the Shaping of Christianity* (New York: Penguin Books, 2007).

[21] Karen Armstrong, *A History of God* (London: Vintage Books, 1999).

[22] https://www.theguardian.com/commentisfree/belief/2009/jul/16/daniel-dennett-belief-atheism

Image credits

Figure 1 – Job
www.holyspiritspeaks.org

Figure 2 – Noah's ark
https://medium.com/@heather.n.hocking, Heather Hocking, 9 July 2018. Last accessed on 21 September 2021.

Figure 3 – Adam & Eve
Ape-Man: The Story of Human Evolution, Robin MacKie, 2000, BBC. An artist's impression of a hominid couple, American Museum of Natural History, Hall of Human Origins, New York (photo alteration by the author).

Figure 4 – Hominid family tree
Courtesy ScienceMe

Figure 5 – Giraffes
PxHere

Figure 6 – Taj Mahal
Bruwer Swanepoel

Figure 7 – Foie gras
Courtesy Éthique & Animaux, Wikimedia Commons

Figure 8 – Brain evolution
Courtesy Scientific American, *Your Brain Evolved from Bacteria* by Dwayne Godwin and Jorge Cham, 1 July 2014.

Figure 9 – A star
Courtesy Space Place_NASA Science

Figure 10 – Tree of life
Courtesy ScienceMe

Figure 11 – Black holes

Figure 12 – Handprints
Courtesy Mariano, Wikimedia Commons

Figure 13 – The first God image (The Sorcerer)
Sketch by Abbé Henri Breuil, courtesy Don's Maps

Acknowledgements

When the Covid-19 pandemic first disrupted our world at the beginning of 2020 and the first lockdown forced us to slow down, I used the opportunity to pen My Religion Story as a short essay. I suspected that it would be controversial, and to test the waters, I gave the paper to a handful of friends and family. My suspicions were confirmed. The few responses received varied widely, from an icy but courteous "thank you" to an "I cannot understand why you delved so deeply into something so mundane". I thought that was a good start. I then sent it to the founder of the Nuwe Hervorming Network, Professor Sakkie Spangenberg. He encouraged me to put the essay on the internet, expand on it, and present it as a short autobiography. Sakkie was also kind enough to read the first draft of the chapters and provided some pointers on proceeding.

I was recommended to Yvonne Shapiro for proofreading. She did a lot more than proofreading and went through my manuscript three times. I am most grateful to her for walking the extra mile. Sarie Potter did a great job researching my images, obtaining approvals where necessary andefining the credits. Nelmarie Swanepoel came up with the printed book cover sketch, which I thought was extraordinary as it captured the essence of my religious journey and confirmed the title. The Christian cross is disintegrating, splintering off, and completing the circle by flowing into the atheist symbol with the rising sun witnessing and approving the process. Sally Rumball made a painting of the sketch, which Adam Rumball of Sharkbuoys Designs turned into an exceptional book cover. Any other typesetter would have walked away from me, but Leah Marais was very patient with me, doing the typesetting as well as providing editing support, and helped me along the independent publishing route.

Annemarie Heymans was the first friend, emerging entirely out of the blue from my religious background, who discovered My Religion Story on the internet and, after having read it, contacted me and provided encouragement and motivation to persevere and complete the book. I am more than indebted to her as she also suggested the title. Karien Coertzen read chapter after chapter as I completed them and kept inspiring me to carry on and finish the book. My wife Elvira Swanepoel supported me unconditionally, without ever having read my essay or the manuscript. She was never a believer and tried her very best to understand what the excitement was all about.

Index

A

Adam and Eve   56, 57, 73, 121, 122, 123, 124, 125, 126, 128
Africa   ii, viii, ix, 3, 7, 11, 16, 17, 22, 23, 24, 25, 30, 33, 34, 52, 56, 60, 61, 66, 69, 71, 72, 85, 103, 133, 135, 136
Afrikaner   i, viii, ix, 1, 13, 16, 17, 25, 30, 34, 69, 136
afterlife   v, ix, 34, 36, 37, 40, 98
agriculture, agricultural revolution   vi, 59, 71, 72, 73, 75
America   18, 21, 50, 72, 136
Andries Pretorius Laerskool   4
army   v, viii, 14, 15, 33, 42
Asiatic mouflon   73
Aslan, Reza   47, 73, 121, 136

B

bacteria, cyanobacteria   65, 91, 138
bees   62, 68
Bethlehem   39
Bible   v, vi, viii, ix, x, 7, 10, 11, 21, 25, 30, 31, 32, 33, 34, 35, 36, 37, 39, 40, 41, 43, 44, 46, 47, 50, 54, 93, 96, 116, 117, 118, 130, 133, 134, 135
Biblecor   viii, 31, 43
Big Bang   vi, 58, 64, 65, 105, 106, 107, 108, 110, 111, 132, 136, 137
black hole   x, 104, 113, 114, 115, 116, 132
Body of Christ   10, 55
born-again   11, 55, 56
Bosman, Dan   25, 27
Breuil, Henri   121, 125, 126, 138
Brits   6, 8, 9, 11, 78. See also Brits High School, Brits hotel
Bruno, Giordano   64
Buddhist   45, 71
Bush, George W   17

C

Caesar, Julius 94
Caledon River 2, 4
Cambrian 68, 91, 92, 112
carbon 79, 80, 91, 103, 109, 111, 112
Catholic, Catholic Church and Catholicism 12, 13, 21, 25, 33, 64, 105, 117, 122, 136
chimpanzees 57, 58, 62, 93
Christian Byzantine Empire 19
Christianity 7, 11, 19, 21, 22, 25, 34, 39, 41, 43, 55, 56, 63, 64, 99, 116, 117, 122, 137, 139
class of '69 7
cloud 44, 48, 100
cognitive, Cognitive Revolution 59, 61, 62, 131
Confessions of Faith 31, 39
Constantine, emperor 43, 117
conversion v, vii, ix, 56, 97
Copleston, Frederick 97
Crimea 20

D

Damascene 116
Damascus 56
Dawkins, Richard 52, 70, 80, 81, 84, 134, 136, 137
De LaPlace, Simon-Pierre 99
Denisovans 60
descent 44, 60, 61
DNA 17, 57, 60, 75, 80, 92, 112
domesticated, domestication 71, 72, 73, 75, 96
Doornfontein viii, 30
Drummond, Henry 99
Druyan, Ann 80, 137
Dutch Reformed Church iii, viii, 16, 22, 30, 31, 32, 38, 39, 50, 52, 53, 54

E

Earth vi, x, 50, 59, 63, 64, 65, 68, 72, 78, 79, 80, 81, 83, 91, 92, 93, 95, 98, 100, 103, 104, 108, 110, 111, 112, 132

Eastern Orthodox Church   19, 122
Edleen   viii, 30, 31, 32, 41, 54
element   107, 109, 110
Enki   47, 48, 49
Enlil   47, 48, 49
entropy   98, 105, 106, 107
Europe   v, viii, 12, 17, 19, 24, 25, 44, 50, 54, 60, 134, 135
Evangelicals   21, 136
event horizon   113, 114
Exorcist, The   24

F

faith   v, vi, vii, viii, ix, 11, 14, 15, 19, 25, 26, 27, 31, 33, 34, 38, 40, 41,
    43, 50, 51, 52, 53, 54, 55, 56, 63, 93, 130, 131, 132, 133, 134
faith healing   viii, 27, 50, 131
father   v, 1, 2, 4, 11, 15, 25, 28, 29, 30, 43, 51, 52, 69, 94, 118, 119, 127
Ficksburg   2, 3, 4, 69
fiction, fictional stories   ix, 52, 62, 63, 120, 128
Foie gras   77, 138
footprints   56, 57

G

Galilei, Galileo   64
Germany   11, 12, 13, 54, 135
Gideons International   v, ix, 11, 33, 54
giraffes   66, 67, 68
God-of-the-Gaps   vi, x, 99, 101
Gospel of Judas   vi, 118, 119, 137
grandmother   v, vii, 2, 3, 4, 58, 86
gravitational   100, 101, 105, 106, 107, 108, 109, 114, 115
gravity   80, 99, 100, 104, 105, 107, 109, 110, 113, 115, 116
Greek philosophy   45
Greene, Brian   106, 137
Guth, Alan   106

H

Harari, Yuval Noah   ix, 58, 62, 72, 74, 129, 132, 133, 136
helium   82, 100, 108, 109

Herr Augustin   11, 12
Herstigte Nasionale Party   22
Hindu   45, 71, 120
Hitchens, Christopher   15, 71, 118, 120, 129, 132, 136
Holy Scripture   64
Holy Spirit   32, 52, 53, 93, 117
Homo erectus   60
Homo sapiens   vi, ix, 59, 60, 61, 62, 65, 73, 75, 78, 87, 95, 96, 98, 103, 112, 121, 126, 130, 135
hospital   vii, 3, 25, 41
hostel life   vii, 6
Hubble, Edwin   105
hunter   70, 127
Hussein, Sadam   18
hydrogen   79, 82, 100, 103, 107, 108, 109, 110, 111

I

India   45, 50, 71, 85
interconnectedness   vi, 98, 102, 113
Islam   44, 45, 120
Israel   ix, 38

J

Jerusalem   v, ix, 38
Jesus   ix, 10, 11, 24, 25, 27, 29, 32, 33, 34, 39, 40, 43, 44, 46, 52, 55, 93, 117, 119, 120, 131
Jesus Christ Superstar   24
Jews   29, 120, 135
Job   34, 35, 36, 138

K

Kazakhstan   19
Khrushchev, Nikita   20

L

Language   vi, 16, 17, 59, 60, 61, 62, 63, 65, 66, 68, 94, 96, 112
Leakey, Mary   56

Lemaître, George   105, 136
Lord of Beasts   126

M

MacLean, Paul   88, 89, 91
Marais, Dr Willie   50
Marais, Jaap   23
Maroela Hostel   16, 23
matric, Grade 12   6, 7, 8, 9, 11, 14
meningitis   3, 10
Milky Way   103, 104, 109, 114
mother, my   v, viii, 2, 10, 11, 15
mycelium   65, 66, 67

N

National Party   16, 22, 23, 29
NATO   20
Nazareth   39
Neanderthals, Homo Neanderthalensis   60
New Testament   37
Newton, Sir Isaac   99, 100, 101, 102, 105, 107
Nuwe Hervorming Netwerk   v, 54

O

Old Testament   iii, 34, 36, 52, 118
Omen, The   25
origin of life   80
osteoarthritis   50
oxygen   79, 82, 91, 92, 103, 109, 111, 112

P

pact with God   14
Parachute Battalion, Parabats   14
Patriarch Kirill   18
police   1, 12, 33
Pope Francis   64
Pope John Paul II   64

Pope Pius Xll   64
Pretoria Gardens   1
Pretoria West   4, 5
primordial   79, 80, 83, 105, 137
promises   v, ix, 30, 37, 38, 40, 41, 42, 43, 49
Protestant   7, 13, 21, 33, 39, 65, 117
Putin, Vladimir   18, 19, 20, 21, 136

R

replicator   vi, 80, 81, 83, 91, 112
Republican   17, 21
Revelation   25, 44, 93
Robertson, Mr   78
rock art   123, 124
Rosemary's Baby   25
Russell, Bertrand   97
Russia   viii, 18, 19, 20, 60
Russian Orthodox Church   18

S

Sagan, Carl   68, 86, 88, 104, 137
Samurai crabs   vi, 85
SARS-CoV-2   85
Satan   24, 25, 34, 35, 36
Saviour   11, 34, 40
sceptic   viii, 26, 29
School   9, 31
Scientific Revolution   59
Second Law of Thermodynamics   vi, 97, 98, 105, 107, 113
Seefeld   12
Skeerpoort   2, 70
Smuts, Jan   16
Socrates   63
Sorour, Mr   3
soul   127, 128
Soviet Union   20
Spangenberg, Izak   iii, 54, 139
Stalin, Josef   19, 134

stardust   x, 100, 112
St Augustine of Hippo   63
storytelling   62, 70, 87
Sumerian   49
Sunday school   3, 5
Supernova   78, 110, 115, 116

T

Taj Mahal   70, 71, 138
Tartar Mongols   20
tithing   30, 40
Toker, Daniel   89, 137
Tree of life   111, 138
Trinity God   ix, x, 32, 45, 52, 117
Triune Brain Hypothesis   88, 89
Trump, Donald   21
turning point   v, 41, 43

U

Ukraine   19, 20
universe   vi, x, 1, 58, 59, 64, 78, 79, 82, 89, 93, 96, 97, 98, 99, 102, 103, 104, 105, 106, 107, 108, 111, 113, 114, 115, 116, 132, 136, 137
University of Chicago   79
University of Pretoria   viii, ix, 15, 32
University of the Witwatersrand   16

V

Van Staden, Mr   94
Van Wyk, Mr   9
Via Dolorosa   v, ix, 38
Vikings   20
virgin birth   44, 46
virus   85
Volp caves   121, 125, 126

www.ingramcontent.com/pod-product-compliance
Lightning Source LLC
Chambersburg PA
CBHW031251290426
44109CB00012B/534